ROMAN

SURREY

ROMAN
SURREY

DAVID BIRD

TEMPUS

First published 2004

Tempus Publishing Ltd
The Mill, Brimscombe Port
Stroud, Gloucestershire GL5 2QG
www.tempus-publishing.com

British Library Cataloguing in Publication Data.
A catalogue record for this book is available from the British Library.

ISBN 0 7524 2889 6

Typesetting and origination by Tempus Publishing.
Printed and bound in Great Britain.

CONTENTS

PREFACE AND ACKNOWLEDGEMENTS

At some time in the year AD 43 the area that is now Surrey became part of the Roman Empire, and remained so for about another 360 years. This book aims to explore what Surrey was like when Britain was part of the Roman world, and when the foundation of London created a new and lasting focus with huge implications for the future county. It was the time of Surrey's first towns, first real industry, first made roads, first baths and central heating, first true coinage.

The book is intended particularly for Surrey residents (both in the modern administrative county and in the parts of historic Surrey now in Greater London), and those studying archaeology or members of local history and archaeological societies. I hope it will also be of interest to professionals concerned with Roman Britain and with the archaeology of South-East England. Inevitably, general studies of Roman Britain cannot take much account of local differences, but as a result they produce a misleading picture of homogeneity in the civilian part of the province. My aim here is not to write the history of Britannia with Surrey illustrations, but rather to concentrate on Roman Surrey in the hope that it will illuminate some of the story of Roman Britain, and a part of the history of Surrey. I have found it impossible to avoid the traditional approach by themes; a greater emphasis on the history and on what life was like would have been preferable, but we need far more evidence before this will be an option. The book is to be seen as a starting point; I hope it encourages more research specifically targeted to fill the many gaps in our knowledge. One of its aims is to explore those gaps and challenge assumptions, and as a result much of what is said here can only be regarded as probable or possible. The reader should keep this in mind; new discoveries provoke fresh thinking, which leads to re-examination of old sources and the construction of a new picture. This continual process of discovery and revision is what makes archaeology so fascinating. A hundred years from now our picture of Roman Surrey will be very different.

The book was written in my own time, and the research on which it is based was also carried out in my own time, but obviously I have benefited from my position as Head of Heritage Conservation and Principal Archaeologist at Surrey County Council, both in terms of access to information and the assistance of my colleagues. I was born in Croydon when it was part of Surrey and have been County Archaeologist for many years; I have also taken part in fieldwork on Roman sites all over Britain and beyond. As a result, I have gained a great deal from many people in this time, and others have generously given assistance specifically for this book, providing information as yet unpublished, comment or illustrations. I would like to thank the following for general or specific assistance: Mary Alexander, Professor Alan Bowman, Emily Brants, the late Dr Hugh Chapman, the late Dr Tony Clark, Norman Clarkson, Jonathan Cotton, the late Charles Daniels, Geoffrey Dannell, John Edwards, Graham Evans, Dr Julie Gardiner, Audrey Graham, David Graham, Alan Hall, John Hampton, Rosamond (Viscountess) Hanworth, Jeremy Harte, Dr Martin Henig, Tony Howe, Gary Jackson, Anne Jones, the late Professor Barri Jones, Phil Jones, Brenda Lewis, Dr Frank Meddens, Jackie McKinley, Professor Clive Orton, Giles Pattison, Frank Pemberton, Jeff Perry, Rob Poulton, David Rudling, Dinah Saich, Harvey Sheldon, David Stokes, Barry Taylor, Margot Walshe, Dr John Peter Wild and David Williams. It would also be appropriate to recognise that a book such as this arises from the work of many others long since dead. I hope I have acknowledged this debt adequately in the introductory chapter. I owe special thanks to Surrey Archaeological Society for permission to reproduce illustrations from their publications. The Society will celebrate its 150th anniversary in 2004, and I hope that this book will be a fitting contribution.

A large part of whatever value the book may have is owed to Brian Wood and his digital wizardry. He has not only provided new photographs but has also improved many of the old illustrations reused here. His work on the illustrations speaks for itself, although he cannot of course be held responsible for the quality of some of the original drawings. Audrey Graham kindly improved several of my own drawings to a far higher standard. Finally, I owe a huge debt to Joanna, my wife, not just for putting up with the long process of writing and production but also for the benefit of encouragement and advice over many years, based on her own extensive knowledge about many aspects of Roman Britain and the Empire, and particularly about religion and Roman objects, both generally and specifically from Roman Surrey.

I should stress that none of these people can be held responsible for my errors, and the opinions expressed are entirely my own.

THE ILLUSTRATIONS

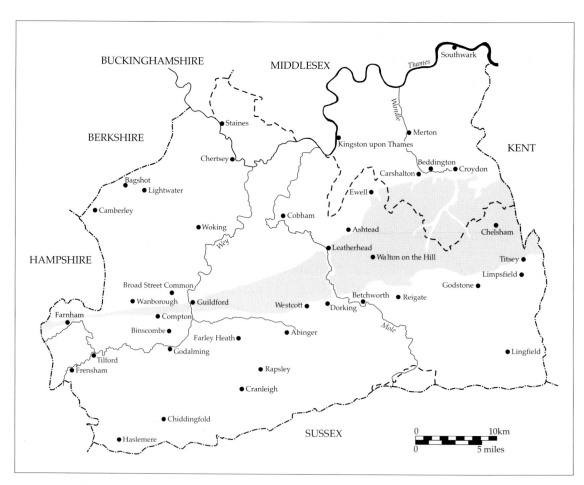

1 Surrey: the location of major places mentioned in the text. The shaded area is the chalk outcrop (ignoring superficial deposits). The dashed lines show recent changes to the county boundary: the area around Staines has been added while a substantial part of the north-east and a small area around Gatwick have been taken away. *Drawing: Audrey Graham*

ONE

INTRODUCTION AND HISTORY OF THE SUBJECT

Although this book has the title 'Roman Surrey', it is not strictly a meaningful expression, as Surrey did not exist in the Roman period. The situation is further complicated because the historic county reached right up to the Thames opposite the City of London. The London boroughs of Southwark, Lambeth, Wandsworth, Richmond, Merton, Croydon, Sutton, and Kingston have been lost to the modern administrative county, which has however gained the Borough of Spelthorne, formerly part of Middlesex *(1)*. To provide continuity with past studies but also recognise present circumstances, the area covered in this book will be both the modern and the historic counties.

Although not a Roman administrative unit this area is reasonably coherent and worthy of study. It is an important part of the surroundings of London, which cannot be properly understood without reference to its hinterland. Surrey is frequently overlooked in more general studies and, in common with the South-East in general, is often treated as just another part of civilian Roman Britain. The region is however very different, as a result of the Weald and its associated topography and soils (see chapter 6). In general terms we can argue that in the Roman period Surrey had a relatively low population and a high percentage tree cover. It is important to remember that the area's high modern population is the result of the coming of the railways and the expansion of London.

Roman Surrey is worthy of study in its own right, as part of a process of understanding localities so that we can reassess and refine our picture of the Roman province as a whole. Surrey also has nationally important sites, although these are sometimes attributed to other counties (such as Farley Heath to Sussex), or even worse, ignored. Sometimes Surrey has led, as with Captain Lowther's pioneering study of relief-patterned flue-tiles, or the successful campaign to change the law as a consequence of the sustained looting of the religious site at Wanborough *(73)*. This place yielded the greatest concentration of Iron Age and Roman gold and silver coins ever found in Britain, as well as a unique set of bronze priestly regalia. It is one of a highly important group of Roman religious sites in the Surrey countryside, some of them discovered very recently. The county also has great potential for achieving a better understanding of the process by which Roman Britain became Saxon England.

> Many a day have I whiled away
> Upon hopeful Farley-heath,
> In its antique soil digging for spoil
> Of possible treasure beneath;
> For, Celts, and querns, and funereal urns,
> And rich red samian ware,
> And sculptured stones, and centurion's bones
> May all lie buried there!
> How calmly serene, and glad have I been
> From morn to eve to stay,
> My Surrey serfs turning the turfs,
> The happy live-long day;
> With eye still bright, and hope yet alight,
> Wistfully watching the mould,
> As my spade brings up fragments of things
> Fifteen centuries old!

Thus (and for several more verses) Martin Tupper, friend of Gladstone, in 1847. The poem finishes 'O, have I not found in that rare ground / A mine of more than wealth!'. Although a poor archaeologist, Tupper's heart was in the right place, for he was searching for information, not treasure. He was probably the first to undertake the systematic excavation of a Roman site in Surrey, although his methods left a great deal to be desired. Antiquarians such as Aubrey, Leland and Stukeley had been noting discoveries of Roman buildings and objects over roughly the previous two hundred years, but their records are usually frustrating in the lack of precision both as to the find itself and its exact location. From about the middle of the nineteenth-century archaeological techniques began to improve, and the new attitudes are seen with the foundation of the Surrey Archaeological Society in 1854. The Society provided a means of coordinating research on the county's archaeology and preserving its finds, and its *Collections* series made possible publication of the results. Thus the second volume included the first meaningful report on the remains of the Roman villa on Walton Heath *(2)*, which had been disappearing over the previous 150 years firstly as a source of material for house-building and road-mending and then at the hands of over-enthusiastic antiquarians. Even the new attitudes could not save the mosaic floor *(colour plate 6)*, which was said to have 'perished from neglect and wanton damage' by the beginning of the twentieth century. It was at least recorded, which is more than can be said for the mosaic removed from the Broad Street Common villa to Clandon House in the early nineteenth century and never seen again.

At about the same time that Tupper was working at Farley Heath, Hugh Diamond was making the first record of Roman Ewell, listing the contents of some of the chalk shafts there *(24)* and making a reasonable attempt at interpretation. Diamond was a pioneer photographer and it is unfortunate that

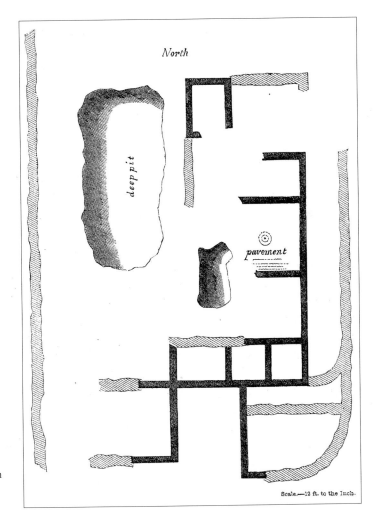

2 Plan of the Walton Heath villa. *From Pocock, 1864*

East.

West.

Open trench.

3 Section of the Abinger villa. *From Darwin 1888, fig 8*

it was just too early for him to make a photographic record of the finds in situ. He does, however, provide a very early example of involving science in archaeology. Intrigued by the discovery of a green-glazed thin-walled vessel, decorated with stripes of white or pale yellow, he had it tested by Michael Faraday of the Royal Institution, who declared it to be a lead glaze. Another very famous scientist, Charles Darwin, became involved in Surrey's Roman archaeology in the 1870s when studying the part played by worms in the burial of ancient buildings (his book on the subject could be read with profit even by today's archaeologists). Darwin arranged for a section to be cut across the recently discovered remains of the Roman villa at Abinger and in so doing gives us a clear record of the destruction caused by the early archaeologists *(3)*. The section shows that the site was excavated by trenches cut alongside the walls with the result that the evidence for the link between floor levels and walls has been removed. This link is crucial to archaeologists: finds from below the floor must pre-date it, and if the floor can be shown to be later than the wall then a date can be suggested for the wall as well. Other similar relationships can then be used to refine the dating and make possible the construction of a phased sequence of activity at a long-lasting site such as a villa or a site in a town. Darwin's section is the earliest from a Roman site in Surrey and is contemporary with ones made by the man regarded as the father of British archaeology, General Pitt Rivers, when he was excavating at nearby barrows in Merrow and Worplesdon.

The best nineteenth-century excavation was carried out by Granville Leveson-Gower on the Roman villa in Titsey Park. It was well recorded for its day (*4; colour plates 15, 16*) and promptly published. It is not surprising that the excavator did not fully understand the site, but he tried to extract as much information as he could, having the soil sifted for finds and examining the animal bones. In this he provided a better record than Lowther, excavating more than 60 years later. Leveson-Gower was active in the area for many years and also examined the Titsey temple, although he did not understand it as such. The large building complex at Chiddingfold (*33*), although excavated in the 1880s, remained unpublished until recently, so the Titsey villa was the best-known Roman building in the county at the beginning of the twentieth century. By then it was clear that there was a substantial settlement in Southwark, where many sites could be listed, even as far south as the recently discovered Tabard Square complex. In contrast, little was known of Ewell or Staines, and only one religious site had been recognised, the Farley Heath temple (Diamond's ritual shafts in Ewell were usually dismissed as rubbish pits). The roads were tolerably well-known and there were a few burial sites, coin hoards and one or two pottery kilns. Soon after 1900 another kiln near Farnham was the subject of a very fine record by the architect Harold Falkner (*59*).

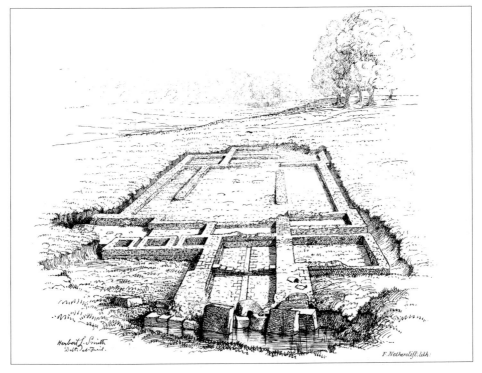

4 Perspective drawing of the 1864-5 excavation of the Titsey villa. *From Leveson-Gower, 1869*

Just before the First World War another villa was found at Compton *(49, 50)* and excavated by Mill Stephenson, who had been involved with the major project at Silchester. In subsequent years up to the middle of the twentieth century there were several new discoveries and some better understanding of sites already known. In roughly chronological order the most important were as follows (with the director's name in brackets): the Ashtead villa and tileworks (A.W.G. Lowther) *(43, 44)*; Farley Heath (Lowther, S.E. Winbolt and R.G. Goodchild at various times); work on Stane Street and in Ewell (Winbolt and Lowther); the Wykehurst Farm tileworks (Goodchild while still at school) *(56)*; the Walton on the Hill villa (Lowther and S.S. Frere) *(47, 48)*; the Chatley Farm bath-house (Frere); work on possible 'villages' and field systems south of Croydon (a young Brian Hope-Taylor); early post-War rescue work by Kathleen Kenyon in Southwark (Frere was nearly arrested as an enemy agent while carrying out a preparatory survey of bombed sites in 1944-5); the Farnham villa (Lowther) *(39, 40, 41)*; pottery kilns at Overwey near Tilford (a young Tony Clark) *(60)*; the synthesis of his own and all other work on roads in Surrey and beyond by I.D. Margary (published as *Roman Ways in the Weald*).

Several of those mentioned were or became important figures in Romano-British archaeology or archaeology more generally. Unfortunately standards varied considerably, with Winbolt probably the worst. The key figure was obviously Lowther, who was born in 1901, and grew up with sufficient money to pursue his interests as he chose. In 1924 he began architectural studies in London (qualifying in 1929) and acted as a volunteer observer of archaeological remains found in the course of building works. In 1926 he began excavations at Ashtead *(5)*, continuing until 1928. He dug with Mortimer Wheeler at Verulamium in 1932 and seems to have been personally responsible for digging the theatre and restoring it for public display. He was commissioned into the army in 1940 but invalided out having contracted polio in the Middle East. As can be seen, Lowther worked on several important Roman sites in Surrey but he was also responsible for work on sites of other periods, such as the Guildown Saxon cemetery, and in particular recorded many archaeological finds in the area around his home in Ashtead.

Lowther seems to have learnt archaeological techniques as he went along. Photographs of the work at Ashtead *(5, 52)* indicate little advance on the techniques used at Abinger in the 1870s. It is important to realise that archaeological excavation carried out in this way will have made it impossible to recognise the traces of any late use of the site, or the subtleties of different floor levels and their relationship with walls. Lowther found one or two complete pots at the site which he thought had been buried as foundation deposits, but it is obvious that excavation carried out using the methods seen in these photographs will have made it impossible to be sure that the pots were actually below a floor level rather than cut into it. His methods improved over time, but internal inconsistencies in published reports indicate that he sometimes

5 Contemporary view of the Ashtead bath-house excavation. *Courtesy Leatherhead Museum*

changed his mind about dating or the relationship between one feature or another which means that the reports must always be treated with care. As none of the original records seems to have survived, these published reports are our only source of information.

What may have been lost in the earlier excavations is shown by Rosamond Hanworth's excavation of the villa at Rapsley in the 1960s. Much more careful excavation made possible the recovery of a phased sequence of development of the site (36), and the recognition of timber buildings. In the second half of the twentieth century much more use could also be made of scientific methods of discovery and the study of the finds, including evidence for the contemporary environment of the sites and details of ancient diet. Analysis of aerial photographs is difficult in Surrey because of the ground conditions, but at least one villa has been found in this way (32) and an extensive field system is known around Mickleham; geophysical survey has also been used with effect as in the discovery of a second villa at Titsey. We now have better details of diet and the environment from studies in Staines and Southwark and detailed analysis of tile fabrics is beginning to throw light on the workings of the tile industry.

It is unfortunately rare to find surviving ancient wood in excavations, but conditions in Southwark are sometimes suitable for wood preservation (26).

Where an adequate piece of wood with enough rings and the sapwood can be found, it is now possible to obtain very accurate dates indeed, and as a result in 1983 a chronology for timbers found in Southwark was constructed covering the years 252 BC-AD 255. This bridged a gap in chronologies prepared from Irish bog oaks and therefore played an important part in establishing a long chronology for European oak that stretches back to around 5000 BC. One result of the work in Southwark was to date the original construction of the large stone building at 15-23 Southwark Street to close to AD 75, on the basis of the felling dates (AD 72, 73 and 74) of piles which had been driven in to the wet ground, still with their bark on, to provide a sturdy base for the building's foundations.

The period from the 1960s and especially the 1970s has seen the development of modern professional rescue archaeology in a desperate attempt to save archaeological evidence in the face of ever-increasing change. Rescue archaeology is not new. Most early discoveries were made as a result of some destructive activity, but it is much easier to deal with a threat such as that posed by the extension of a kitchen garden at Compton than something like a modern town centre redevelopment. The main threats come about as a result of mechanisation because it is now so easy to shift large areas of soil around: they include development-related activities such as offices, houses, new roads, golf courses and mineral extraction, but land management such as forestry, agriculture and heathland restoration can also cause problems.

Planning policies are now in place in an attempt to ensure that archaeological remains are given appropriate consideration in the course of development, but it remains difficult to safeguard sites from activities such as farming and treasure hunting. The latter is particularly worrying because important sites are specifically targeted (information about sites to loot is actually made available on the internet!) and only a very few greedy people are needed to cause serious archaeological damage. It is a matter for concern that archaeologists are unable to publicise some sites as a result. Probably the most notorious example of treasure hunting anywhere in Britain was at Wanborough, where dozens of people descended on the site from all over the country to loot thousands of Iron Age and Roman coins and sell them to unscrupulous dealers who then dispersed them to others all over the world. The looters hacked knowingly through the remains of Roman buildings and even damaged and threw away unique Roman bronze objects (73). Two major archaeological excavations had to be mounted in order to rescue archaeological information before it was destroyed.

The damage at Wanborough was so obvious that a campaign initiated by Surrey Archaeological Society resulted in a new law, the Treasure Act (1996). The name is unfortunate as it implies a link with treasure hunters, but these have always been a small and mindless minority, to be distinguished from responsible metal detectorists. In fact, following the new Act, Finds Liaison

Officer posts have been established and it has become much easier for detectorists to report their discoveries. Those who record their finds very carefully have produced important results from their own fieldwork, for instance in the Godstone area, and when working with archaeologists, as recently at Wanborough itself, Frensham, Westcott and Ewell. There, they have ensured a much better rate of recovery of metal objects from archaeological excavations.

Rescue archaeology has been particularly important in town centres (*19, 20*) and where large areas of the countryside are taken for developments *(9, 30)*. A simple list of new sites or others where there have been significant advances very recently indicates the pace of new discoveries: Wanborough (new temple); Chelsham, Carshalton, Cranleigh (new villas); Frensham, Westcott, Betchworth (new religious sites); new information from Southwark, Staines, Ewell, Croydon, Dorking; important rural evidence from the Tongham/ Runfold area, Thorpe Lea, Wey Manor Farm. It has become difficult to assimilate the evidence, and the reader should keep in mind that it might only take one or two new sites to alter considerably the picture of Roman Surrey presented in this book.

TWO

INVASION AND AFTERMATH

Southern Britain was brought firmly into the orbit of the Roman world as a result of the campaigns of Julius Caesar in the mid-first century BC. In his history of the conquest of Gaul, Caesar states that there were direct links between Gallic and British tribes, even to the extent of being ruled by the same person. Some of the tribal names are repeated on both sides of the Channel, including that of the Atrebates, whose area of influence probably included at least part of Surrey, as the preponderance of Atrebatic coins at Wanborough suggests (although these are of a somewhat later date). In the nineteenth century some writers thought that Caesar's second expedition to Britain in 54 BC passed through the county. The first edition of the Ordnance Survey 6 inches to the mile map, published in 1872, even carries the inscription 'British Camp occupied by Caesar before the crossing of the Thames at the Cowey Stakes' written across the Iron Age hillfort at St George's Hill, Weybridge (6). There is no reason to suppose that this is true; Caesar is more likely to have crossed the Thames further downstream and headed up the natural routeway of the Lea valley. The 'Cowey Stakes', near Walton Bridge, were probably the remains of a post-Roman fish weir, or a line of stakes marking the line of a ford, rather than the sharpened stakes designed to protect the crossing place that the Britons are said to have used in an unsuccessful attempt to stop Caesar's legions. It has been suggested that some of the Surrey hillforts on the edge of the Weald (Anstiebury, Holmbury and Hascombe) were strengthened or occupied in response to a perceived threat from Caesar, but this is also unlikely. These forts still survive within the landscape, but St George's Hill Camp has succumbed to

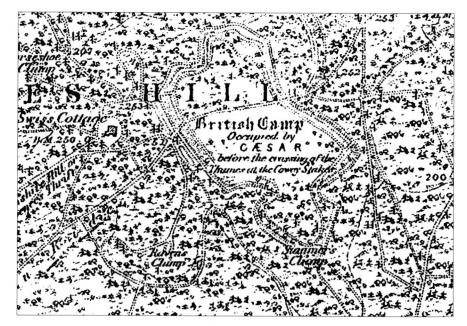

6 Caesar was here! Extract from the 1872 Ordnance Survey map showing the hillfort on St George's Hill

one of the curses of modern Surrey, the gated housing estate, in spite of the valiant attempts of Surrey Archaeological Society in the early twentieth century.

Caesar's campaign of 54 BC ended in defeat for Cassivellaunus, who was the leader of a tribal grouping north of the Thames. Terms were imposed involving the giving of hostages and the annual payment of tribute and from that time onwards it is probable that ever closer links developed between the tribes of southern Britain and the expanding Roman Empire. Unfortunately we have little written evidence for the next hundred years, and it is always difficult to use archaeology to provide details of specific events. It is thought likely that two major tribal groupings emerged, one north of the Thames with centres of power at places like Verulamium (near St Albans) and Camulodunum (around Colchester), the other south of the river with centres near Chichester and Silchester. These groupings are usually referred to as the eastern and southern kingdoms or the Catuvellauni and the Atrebates respectively. Both of them had links with Rome, perhaps quite specifically so in the sense that young British men of 'noble' birth grew up there as hostages, given the same upbringing as upper class Romans. When these men returned to their tribes in due course, probably around the time of the first Roman Emperor, Augustus, the coinage they issued has been analysed to suggest the influence of their education. This did not prevent a power struggle developing between the eastern and the southern kingdoms, as well as internal struggles within them; both gave rise to suppliants fleeing to the Romans. The last of these was Verica, the ruler of the Atrebates, apparently driven out by the actions of the Catuvellauni or their allies, and his flight provided the excuse for the Roman invasion of AD 43.

Claudius was the new Roman Emperor, installed in AD 41 following the assassination of his predecessor, Gaius (usually known as Caligula), and it is generally accepted that he was in need of a military triumph to consolidate his position. This is not the place for a detailed discussion of the campaign, which has been the subject of fresh thinking in recent years, but some aspects are of interest here because it is possible that part of the campaign took place in Surrey. Whichever way the invasion worked it is likely that Roman forces under the future Emperor Vespasian (then commanding Legio II Augusta) crossed the county *(7)*. Our main source of evidence is the history written by Cassius Dio many years after the event, but his account has very few geograph- ical details (although modern text books sometimes imply the opposite). A story has become established that the Roman army landed at Richborough in Kent and then fought a battle at a crossing of the Medway before a second action at a crossing of the Thames, probably near London. The army then supposedly waited there for Claudius before proceeding to a final defeat of the Britons on the way to Colchester, where symbolically a major army base was established. It is, however, possible to argue that the main landing was in the area of the Solent, with a base near Chichester and in due course another base established at or near Silchester. From here part of the final advance of the initial campaign would have been through what is now Surrey. Rather than on the Medway, the famous river battle may actually have been on a Surrey river, such as the Wey or the Wandle (the latter is not much noticed these days, within the heavily built up area south-west of London, but in its day it was

7 Dupondius of Vespasian (IMP CAES VESPASIAN AVG COS III [=AD 71]). From Norman Clarkson's collection; there is a similar coin from Farley Heath. *Photograph: Brian Wood*

strong enough to power many mills). The river battle story relies entirely on Dio's narrative, and this actually makes a battle on the Medway unlikely, for we are told that the Romans landed unopposed and that the Britons were caught unprepared. In these circumstances there is every reason to suppose that, had they landed in Kent, Roman forces would have crossed the Medway well before their enemies appeared in sufficient strength to try to stop them.

In part the argument is between those who think in terms of an almost modern-style invasion, with front lines and the gradual conquest of territory, and those who think more of the way Caesar was able to operate, sometimes with individual forces in all the different corners of Gaul at the same time. It is often forgotten that his first trip to Britain was undertaken from a base in territory controlled by a tribe he had not yet conquered, or that the Romans had allies among the Britons. In fact, it is likely that the Claudian 'invasion' was actually more like a procession, with the Roman forces – four or five times as large as William the Conqueror's army – having difficulty finding a large enough enemy force to fight so as to give Claudius a suitable victory. Even in Caesar's day we are told that some British tribes sent emissaries to offer submission before he had set sail for Britain; around 100 years later it is likely that much of southern Britain had become so much a part of the Roman world that many tribal groups accepted the Roman presence without a fight. There is hardly any evidence for forts anywhere in the South-East, which probably only existed at the main bases such as Richborough, Colchester, Chichester, and Silchester. The Roman army did not conquer territory but peoples; a tribe submitted, if necessary after a battle, and was then expected to provide tribute in some form (usually supplies of food) and hostages. In the north-west of the Empire the provinces were administered through tribal areas, with local government in the hands of the tribal 'upper class'. Sometimes at first allies were rewarded with rather more meaningful self-government, as client kingdoms, and this was probably the case with the Atrebates, perhaps from the beginning under a new king, Cogidubnus (or Togidubnus), given a wide area to rule probably including Sussex, Surrey, Hampshire and even further west.

Certainly, little evidence is known for any Roman military presence in Surrey. Two sites previously claimed as marching camps are now known to be nothing of the kind. Both were originally noted on aerial photographs, on which buried ditches can be seen marked out by parch marks on the grass or lines in a crop. The shapes of the enclosures marked out by the ditches have a superficial resemblance to Roman military works (because they are rectangular with playing card corners), but in each case archaeological excavation has demonstrated that this is not the correct interpretation. One site on the playing field of the Matthew Arnold School near Staines has been shown to be of medieval date, while the other, on a ridge near Westcott, west of Dorking, can now be dated to the Late Iron Age. This site may have had a ritual use, continuing into the Roman period, which could explain the presence of a Roman cavalry pendant found nearby. An early military base has been postulated at Southwark, but this would only make sense in conjunction with London, for the road to the Thames crossing would have required considerable engineering, the crossing itself needed a bridge, and neither would make sense without the establishment of the settlement on the far bank. As it now seems clear that London was not founded until nearer AD 50, up to seven years after the 'invasion', a military explanation makes much less sense. There are, however, several finds of military equipment from Southwark, so it is likely that the army played some role in the building of the road, the bridge and the start of the settlement itself.

It is equally probable that the military had a role in the bridging of the Thames at Staines, on the Silchester–Colchester road, which may well pre-date the foundation of London. The road will have been of major strategic importance in the early years as there were probably legionary bases at each end. The place-name *Pontibus*, 'at the bridges', giving the name in Latin, may suggest that there was no pre-existing crossing (when a name incorporating the British element *-brivae* might be expected). It may even be that the bridge was constructed originally in AD 43 to aid the final drive on Camulodunum (Colchester) under the personal command of Claudius, who is said by Dio to have joined the army where it was already waiting by the Thames, and then led it across the river. A notable find from Staines is part of the cheek piece of a Roman cavalry helmet of the first century AD, but this cannot on its own establish the existence of a military site and there is nothing else from the town to suggest it. Not far from Staines, on the other side of the river, archaeological excavations at the site of the former Petters Sports Field (now partly under the M25) revealed a very straight length of ditch and associated palisade *(8)* apparently with a military style entrance and a bronze military harness mount of mid-first century date that can be paralleled very closely at the early Roman fort site of Hod Hill in the west country. One mount cannot prove the existence of a military site as such, and the ditch cannot be closely dated. If it is a military post it might well be related to the aftermath of the revolt of Boudica, when Roman authority was reimposed and campaigning in the South-East may have been necessary for a short time.

Boudica, traditionally called Boadicea, led a revolt of the Iceni, a tribe in East Anglia of which she was queen, in AD 60/61. The revolt also involved the Trinovantes of Essex and no doubt others from north of the Thames, and initial attempts by Roman military units to suppress the rebels failed with considerable losses. According to the historian Tacitus, the settlements at Colchester, London and Verulamium were sacked and looted. There is evidence from each place for destruction by fire, and it has recently been found in Southwark as well. This may be significant, for it shows that Boudica's forces must have crossed the Thames. The standard theory is that they later made their way north, to meet the surviving elements of the Roman army under the then governor, Suetonius Paulinus, rushing back from campaigning in Wales,

8 Early ditch and palisade trench at Petters Sports Field. *Photograph: author*

and were smashed at a battle in the Midlands. It would make more sense, however, for the battle to have taken place somewhere out towards Silchester. In the first place it is clear that Boudica's forces were bent on destruction and looting; what more likely than that they would head for the growing towns or centres of the resurgent Atrebates, close allies of the Romans and probably seen as an old enemy? We might also expect that Suetonius would have anticipated such an action and would therefore have sought to bring his troops down to protect the towns, especially as they could provide allies to stand with him: he had been reluctant to abandon London. They also represented both his main surviving supply bases and his most trustworthy links back to the Continent: we know from Tacitus that Cogidubnus was honoured for his loyalty to Rome. Suetonius had ordered Legio II, which is believed to have been based at Exeter at this time, to move to join him, so an intended junction of his forces somewhere out west from London would make sense (in the event the legion stayed where it was, its temporary commander duly falling on his sword when this turned out to be the wrong thing to have done). Boudica's final defeat may therefore have been somewhere on the route between London and Silchester and it has even been suggested that it was near Virginia Water, but our only sources give insufficient evidence to be certain of any site, and there is no archaeological evidence for the battle anywhere.

THREE

BECOMING PART OF
THE EMPIRE

In theory, AD 43 marks the change from Iron Age to Roman Britain, but in fact there was probably little change at first for most of the people living in our area. Even the rapid development of Southwark and the making of the first part of the road system is probably to be dated between five and ten years after the so-called invasion.

It is in general difficult to assess the impact of the Empire on the area because Iron Age Surrey is not well understood. There have been a number of important recent discoveries but we need much more evidence, especially away from the river gravels. One area with good evidence for Iron Age settlement is around Tongham and Runfold, east of Farnham. Groups of the round houses typical of the period have been recorded in excavations by the Surrey County Archaeological Unit (9). Over forty of these houses are now known in this area, which is a huge increase in such evidence from the county as a whole. Similar houses are also known on sites near St George's Hill in the Brooklands area and there is evidence for settlement elsewhere on the river gravels as for example at Thorpe Lea Nurseries (30). There is also less well-defined evidence for occupation that seems to be especially related to the chalk of the Downs, typified by the settlement at Hawk's Hill near Leatherhead, where large storage pits are known.

The county has a number of hillforts, with only one exception (War Coppice at Caterham) grouped to north or south of the Downs and not on the chalk itself. They are mostly presumed to be of Iron Age date although there is little evidence for occupation. Defences having more than one rampart, as at St George's Hill (6), may be assumed to date to the Iron Age,

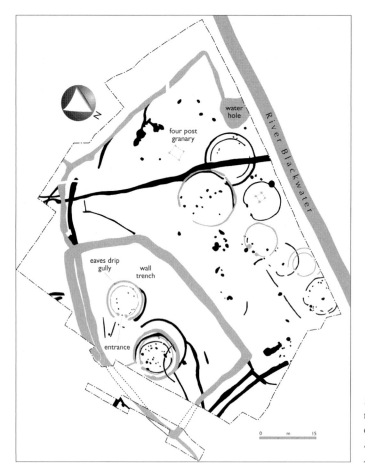

9 Tongham: Iron-Age round houses and enclosures. *Courtesy Surrey County Archaeological Unit*

and excavations at Anstiebury, Felday, Holmbury and Hascombe in the south of the county have produced some Iron Age pottery in every case. This shows that in fact the hillforts may have been in use at different times, Felday in particular being late in the period. The functions of these hillforts are still a matter for debate, but it is generally accepted that those in the south were in some way linked to the seasonal use of the Weald, providing control of the routes and protection for stock and people where necessary.

In the Thames gravels area in and to the north of the county a contrast between evidence for land-use in the Late Bronze Age and afterwards has led J.D. Hill to suggest that there may have been a considerable decline in population, with the area mostly lacking permanent settlement in the mid to late Iron Age. On this model population centres further north may have used the area for transhumance, driving animals in to pasture on a seasonal basis. The offerings to the Thames of high-quality metalwork such as the famous Battersea Shield could be seen as a ritual associated with this process. Surrey's northern hillforts could then be interpreted as part of the system of control, which might perhaps even include those further south.

Archaeological excavations by the Surrey County Archaeological Unit on gravel extraction sites north and south of the Thames in recent years have tended to show that the pattern noted by Hill is relatively true north of the river but that there continue to be Iron Age occupation sites to the south. It may be therefore that whatever caused the changes had less effect in Surrey south of the Thames. It is, however, likely that the population was low, and this may be one reason for the noticeable lack of a major Late Iron Age centre in our area. Such 'oppida' are known for most of the surrounding regions and it has been suggested, on the grounds of coin distribution patterns, that there should be one in the area to the west of London, but nothing has yet been found to indicate such a site.

Another reason for a particularly low population for part of the Iron Age might be a major volcanic event causing dust clouds, recognised through its effect on tree growth, thought to have occurred around 200 BC. Such events have serious implications for crops. Whatever the reasons, there are indications of change in the Late Iron Age, some of which show the increasing influence of ideas from the western Roman Empire in the years following Caesar. The pottery in use in Surrey, and the sources of quernstones, differs between east and west, and has been used to suggest a split in 'tribal' influences along roughly the line of the Mole. As river valleys, especially smaller ones, tend to unite rather than divide, it may be that the split was a little further to the east, along the watershed between the Mole and the Eden. This divide may then have continued into the Roman period.

In general there are indications of continuity from the late Iron Age into Roman times. Sites near Westcott and Betchworth *(10)*, discussed in more detail in a later section, seem to have begun in the first century AD before the 'invasion' and continued into the early Roman period. They appear to represent some of the new approaches to sites of religious significance as a result of influence from Gaul and may also reflect a reaction to the uncertainties of changing times. There are indications of Iron Age activity at the known Roman rural temple sites as well. A group of cremation cemeteries in the south-west of the county span the period of change from late Iron Age to early Roman and evidence from some of the occupation sites also suggests continued occupation with little change. Where there is evidence for the wider landscape, as at Thorpe Lea Nurseries, it can be seen that the pattern of the Iron Age layout is developed into the Roman period *(30)*. There is even early Roman pottery from the hillfort at Anstiebury, enough to suggest some continuity of use for a while.

In due course the Roman period saw the introduction of many new things: a new administrative system, new gods, a new and Empire-wide currency, new roads, new settlement types, new building types, new goods, new plants, new

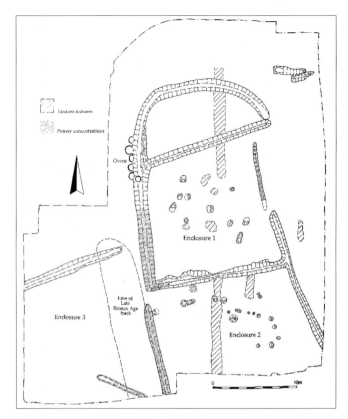

Modern features

Pottery concentrations

Ovens

Enclosure 1

Line of
Late
Bronze Age
track

Enclosure 3

Enclosure 2

0   10m

10 Betchworth: plan of
enclosure. *Drawing: David
Williams*

eating (and drinking) habits, new (or improved) animals, new farming
methods. Such elements as towns, roads and coinage all have pre-Roman
aspects, but there were also very real differences in the Roman period. Towns
were planned, with rectangular buildings, tiled roofs, baths, and so on; roads
were metalled and engineered; coins were used as we would recognise, in a
proper monetary economy, at least in some places. What is difficult to assess is
the degree to which the population as a whole was Romanised; was there a
veneer of 'Roman'-style life in the major towns and villas, or did the changes
penetrate more deeply among the population as a whole?

Roman administration in the west was carried out through the conquered
or allied tribes and relied on each having a chief town to act as a centre; in
Britain these towns had to be created. Some of the 'tribes' were probably artificial divisions of larger groupings, at least in part, and this may have been the
case in our area. As we have seen, at first Surrey may have been within
Cogidubnus' Atrebatic client kingdom and therefore not strictly part of the
Roman province until later in the first century. When this happened, the
kingdom was split between the tribes or *civitates* of the Belgae, the Regni and
the Atrebates, with their 'capitals' at Winchester, Chichester and Silchester

respectively. It is sometimes suggested that Surrey was included in the *civitas* of the Regni but this is unlikely; our main source, the geographer Ptolemy, suggests that the Atrebates and the Cantiaci (the people of Kent) were neighbours and the territory of the Regni was 'below' them. It would make sense if the Weald was treated as a boundary then as it was later on. Surrey was therefore probably largely in the Atrebatic area, but the boundary with the Cantiaci may have been further west than the later Kent/Surrey border. As we have seen, Iron Age pottery suggests such a divide, and later on there were strong links between east Surrey and west Kent in the early Saxon period; the medieval buildings of Tandridge continue this pattern. Canterbury was the chief town of the Cantiaci but Rochester may have served as administrative centre for the western part of the *civitas*. Silchester, south of Basingstoke, was the 'capital' of the Atrebates. It is likely that the area north of the Thames was within the *civitas* of the Catuvellauni and therefore the chief town for the Staines area was probably Verulamium, next to St Albans. It is not clear how London and Southwark fit into this picture, but they were probably part of a freestanding community with no formal role in the surrounding countryside and no formal territory.

It is difficult to assess the changes brought about by the new administrative system, not least because we know very little about what was being replaced. To the ordinary person there may have been little change in practice, especially if the Atrebates were more like an aristocracy controlling an older-established population, as is possible. The new tribal councils based at the 'capital' towns were made up of the top people in each *civitas*, who would have been the pre-existing aristocracy or their descendants (especially in those areas which had allied themselves to the Romans). These people were expected to have a stake in the countryside and no doubt acted in some ways like the later landed gentry. In whatever fashion land had been owned in the pre-Roman period it came to be held in ways we would recognise, and there are documents to indicate this, such as the writing tablet from London concerning Julius Bellicus' legal dispute, noted below.

Magistrates were elected from the tribal council to head the local administration. This was a Roman model but probably had antecedents among the tribes of the South-East at least (with their Gaulish links). There would have been some form of more local administration also, with the *civitas* broken down into smaller units called *pagi* (singular *pagus*). The major religious centres may have played a role here, especially as the tribal officials probably officiated as priests at the major ceremonies. When the roadside settlements developed they also must have found a means to take community decisions, whether as formal *vici* (singular *vicus*), which had a legal standing, or in some informal way. Again, the religious centre of such settlements probably had a role to play (and it might be noted that the formal forum of a major town would normally have an associated temple).

The highest authority in the province was the Governor, formally standing in place of the Emperor and set at the head of the military units stationed in Britannia. As a check on his activities financial matters were in the hands of a Procurator who answered directly to the Emperor. Taxes, mostly in the form of provisions for the army, were the responsibility of the tribal councils and so most of the local population in our area may have seen little sight of soldiers or provincial officials once the military bases had been moved to the north and the west, as they were early in the Roman period. As it is clear that corn was already often gathered and stored under central control in the Iron Age there may again have been little difference for the average farmer.

A 'popular' title for this book would have been *The Romans in Surrey,* but this would perpetuate the myth that Britain was somehow occupied by the Romans. It is partly a matter of definition; 'Roman' by this date can only mean Roman citizen, which already covered much of the population of Italy and parts of Spain, Gaul and Germany in the west. The 'Roman' army that entered Britain in AD 43 was composed of units made up of many nationalities, relatively few of them Italian. There may even have been Britons among them.

There will have been Roman citizens in places like Southwark, and we can now name one as Tiberinius Celerianus as a result of a recent discovery *(85)*. Senior, the Staines 'healer' (if that was his name) was probably another citizen *(27)*. It is possible that Roman Londoners may have bought land in the countryside, if that is the correct interpretation to place on the text of a wooden writing tablet found in London, which apparently refers to a legal dispute:

> In the consulship of the Emperor Trajan Hadrian Caesar Augustus for the second time, and Gnaeus Fuscus Salinator, on the day before the Ides of March [14 March 118]. Whereas, on arriving at the property in question, the wood Verlucionium, fifteen *arepennia* more or less, which is in the canton [*civitas*] of the Cantiaci in Dibussu [illegible] parish, [illegible], neighboured by the heirs [of illegible] and the heirs of Caesennius Vitalis and the vicinal road, Lucius Julius Bellicus said that he had bought it from Titus Valerius Silvinus for forty *denarii*, as is contained in the deed of purchase. Lucius Julius Bellicus attested that he [continuation lost]. (Tomlin 1996, 211)

It may be noted that if it is correct that part of our area was in the territory of the Cantiaci, the wood in question may have been in Surrey. Julius Bellicus, Caesennius Vitalis and Valerius Silvinus will all have been Roman citizens. So might G I S, recorded on one of the relief-patterned tiles from the Ashtead tilery *(colour plate 8)*. These letters may have stood for the owner, perhaps Gaius Julius S.....; if so, having three names would mark him as a citizen.

G I S may have been a retired military man to judge from some aspects of the Ashtead site, discussed further below. An elaborate bronze strainer of

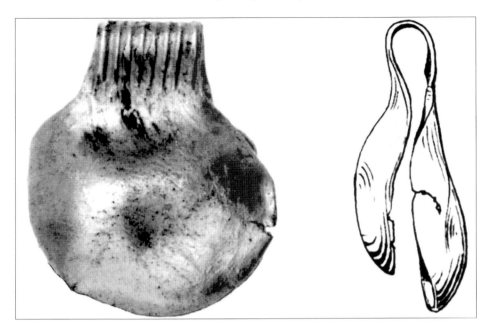

11 Gold *bulla* from Chelsham (about 22mm high). *Photograph courtesy of the British Museum; drawing: David Williams*

military type from near Thorpe is likely to have been deliberately deposited in the Thames as an offering, perhaps when it had become an heirloom, and possibly this also suggests a retired military man of some status. A few other finds from Surrey suggest high-status owners. A worn gold *bulla* of Etruscan or early Roman type comes from somewhere near Chelsham *(11)*; it should have been the personal amulet of a high-ranking Roman child. Further south near Lingfield a heavy gold signet ring ought to have been the property of a Roman knight or even senator. A pottery lamp from near Beddington with an image of the eastern deity Attis has been described as the finest ever found in Britain. Because these finds are unusual it has been suggested that they may have been imported in more modern times, but we have no reason to suppose the presence of a profligate collector scattering ancient finds about east Surrey. Moreover one equally special find came in fragments from a controlled excavation, at the Rapsley villa. This had been a glass cage cup *(12)* and even if old when taken to the site must still have been a very precious possession; there seem to be no other examples known from Britain. That such a rare object could make its way into the depths of the Surrey Weald suggests that we should not too easily dismiss other special finds just because they are discovered by chance.

No large towns were planted in Surrey, and none developed, probably because of the effect of having London/Southwark on the doorstep, although the probably low population of the area will also have had an effect. There are

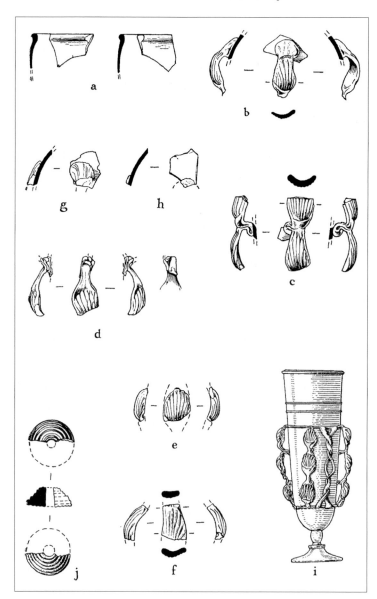

12 Glass from the Rapsley villa; all except 'a' and 'j' come from a cage cup similar to the one shown as 'i'. *From Hanworth 1968, fig 28*

a number of small roadside settlements, however, which seem to have developed spontaneously from about AD 70, as a result of the new trading patterns and markets (and a peaceful environment). The establishment of London must have had an effect both as a market and as a magnet for traffic along the new roads which will have made travel at all times much easier. How much easier can be seen from the situation after they went out of use; later on, travel in some parts of Surrey became very difficult in places, so that diversions of tens of miles might be necessary in order to reach London from the south of the county. Eighteenth- and nineteenth-century map evidence indicates that north of Dorking the Stane Street route was then still in use, presumably because of difficulties with the road along the Mole valley. It has been said that it would have needed courage to drive wheeled vehicles along this road before it was upgraded in 1855. The importance of the new Roman roads is demonstrated by their evident influence on the settlement pattern, especially in the clay areas.

It is difficult to judge the effect on the overall population as a result of the changes. London and Southwark expanded so rapidly in the early years that the bulk of the population must have been incomers, but in due course they may have exerted the pull known in later times. Evidence from the city's cemeteries has been analysed to suggest that the population differed little from that of the rest of Roman Britain but the comparison would usually be with other towns because of the difficulty of finding much evidence for the rural population. It must be likely that the bulk of the population of the roadside settlements, which apparently had no Iron Age predecessors, came from the surrounding countryside, and this raises interesting questions that cannot at present be answered. Was there a growth in the population generally or were some of the sites in the countryside abandoned (with the land perhaps now worked from the new nucleated settlements)?

It seems to have taken around thirty years for the development of the roadside settlements to begin, which suggests that this was the result of a new generation being more in tune with the new ideas and able to seize the opportunities. Presumably the Boudican episode will also have delayed matters, and London/Southwark had to make a fresh start, probably only now taking on the function of provincial capital (although the role probably did not exist officially). Other changes took much longer. Although it is claimed from time to time, there is actually no convincing evidence for the imposition of the regular Roman field system known as centuriation anywhere in Britain. It is only to be expected, if at all, near the *coloniae* like Lincoln, established for veteran legionaries. Where we have actual evidence in our area there is little sign of change in the landscape until about the end of the second century, when more regular field systems were established, at least in places on the gravels *(30)*. One or two of the villas may be earlier but the majority belong to the second century or later. It seems clear that the changes introduced as a result of the events of AD 43 developed gradually and were only sudden in a few instances.

This suggests that Romanisation may have been more than a veneer because it developed from within in response to the outside influences. In this sense it can be seen as a continuation from the Iron Age in the period after Caesar, and indeed before, since Britain has always reacted in its own way to ideas coming from Europe. It is probable that life in villas and towns was more 'Roman', but in Surrey this will have been very much Romano-British. The nature of the roadside settlements and the apparent lack of spectacular villas suggests that

13 Reconstruction of the Rapsley villa in Period V by Cedric de la Nougerede. *From Hanworth 1968, plate 8*

these were mostly local developments. Rapsley's owners may have had a rare glass vessel but neither their villa nor its location in the Weald *(13)* suggests anything out of the ordinary. Heated rooms and baths are of course Roman introductions, but it is not difficult to understand the attraction (especially as I am writing these lines in January). Building types and personal ornaments in Britain are often of the Roman period rather than Roman as such and some things hint at a very real Britishness. For example, there is a type of make-up accessory, the small metal cosmetic grinder, which according to Ralph Jackson is almost an exclusive British product (one Surrey example comes from the Beddington villa). It would be interesting to know what this says about the appearance of Romano-British women.

The Roman 'invasion' brought many changes, but they were probably gradually absorbed into the local culture as part of a continuous process. This process continued throughout the Roman period, so that eventually the fourth century differed markedly from the first.

FOUR

ROADS AND THE LOCATION
OF ROADSIDE SETTLEMENTS

From early in the Roman period the most important sites in the new British province were connected by specially made roads. It is usually held that the initial purpose of these roads was military, for rapid communications and ease of moving troops and supplies, but some of the roads to London may have been built more with trade and the exploitation of the province in mind. Nevertheless, all the major roads were no doubt designed by military engineers, and constructed by the army probably with locally conscripted labour. In the later Roman period in particular the roads in some areas are marked by milestones. None are known in Surrey, a reflection no doubt of the lack of suitable local stone; could there have been wooden posts? Main roads were also provided with so-called 'posting stations' at regular intervals, where official travellers were entitled to free accommodation and fresh horses or mules. They were set at intervals of about 20km, alternating between *mutationes*, where as the name implies horses could be changed, and *mansiones*, where a night's rest might be taken. The word *mansio* is also used of an official inn which would have been expected to provide lodgings and bathing facilities. Because of the needs of travellers and in particular of the animals that provided their motive power, it was usual to site these stations at stream or river crossings whenever possible. This would also have facilitated maintenance of the crossing places, which are likely to have had wooden bridges, or paved fords, although no reliable evidence has yet been found in the county. There should also be evidence for how the animals were managed; associated enclosures are likely to have existed, but they are not usually considered or noted.

It is interesting in this respect to note the recently discovered evidence that in Staines the gravel 'island' to the north of the town and the rich meadows between the 'islands' were used to graze animals and produce hay.

Some of the new roads probably followed roughly the course of a pre-existing route; others were completely new constructions. In both cases they would have been newly surveyed and laid out in straight stretches between aiming points, with appropriate allowance for climbing or descending those obstacles that could not be by-passed. Even here diversions were made by short straight stretches rather than curves, as for example in the climb around Juniper Hill on Stane Street, or north of Titsey on the London–Lewes road. The straight stretches, sometimes preserved by hedgerows, parish boundaries or later roads, are the main clues to the former presence of these Roman roads, perhaps supported by place-name or documentary evidence. Examples in Surrey include Stane Street through Ockley *(colour plate 1)*; Pebble Lane north of Dorking; the London–Lewes road north of Titsey, marked by the course of the former county boundary even including the zig-zag diversion down Skid Hill; and Tilburstow Hill south of Godstone, near the significantly named Stratton ('farm on the street'). Likely road lines tested by excavation normally reveal evidence for deliberate construction and surfacing, almost invariably an indication of Roman date.

There have been several excavations across Roman roads in Surrey, but only a few to modern standards. Older publications usually fail to provide an adequate record of what was actually there. Outside towns roads can leave surprisingly little archaeological evidence. The Surrey evidence in general suggests that road width varies according to location and that it is rare to encounter what seems to be the traditionally accepted standard for a Roman road: the raised 'agger', with side ditches parallel to the road and some distance away on either side. From the sections that have been recorded it seems that the roads were usually around 6m in width with the surviving metalling varying between about 100 and 250mm. Apart from areas where a causeway was appropriate, as in parts of the Weald, the roads usually seem to lack any substantially raised base and ditches are only present where the ground conditions dictate a need for drainage. Probably one factor would be Surrey's topography, where roads often need to be terraced into a slope. In general they have a sub-base of larger stones, flint or greensand, sometimes over a sand layer, with some sort of finer surfacing material over the top, usually pebbles or gravel. It is likely that there were small quarries at regular intervals alongside the roads where they go through suitable country, but these seem rarely to have been recorded or investigated.

In some places the roads survived in use, and the line is reasonably well preserved. In such cases, because of the constant use, it will often be found that the modern road wanders off the original course to either side. It is the idea of the road that is preserved, rather than its exact line. In other places, as noted,

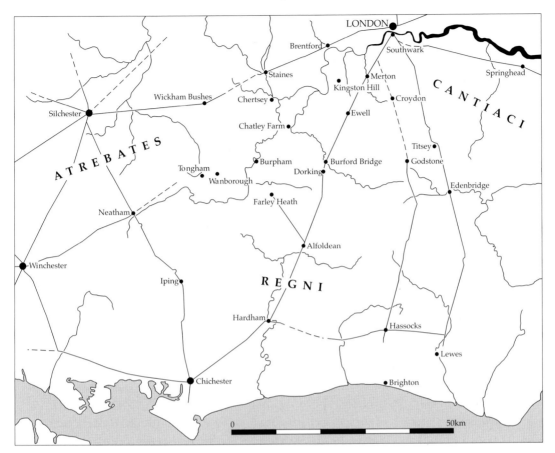

14 Roman roads in Surrey and beyond, and Roman-period tribes. The places named figure in the discussion in the text. *Drawing: Audrey Graham*

later boundaries preserve the line but the road itself has vanished except as an earthwork or a buried feature, when it can only be found by archaeological methods such as aerial photography, geophysical survey or excavation. These factors should be kept in mind when considering, for example, the possible course of the London–Winchester road.

It is rare to be able to date road construction closely, except perhaps in towns. Sometimes a road will seal an earlier site, but it is often not possible to say with certainty how soon after the earlier site was abandoned or destroyed that the road was laid down. It is likely, however, that the main roads in Surrey were all made soon after the 'invasion'. There were probably three such roads, each heading to London, from Chichester, Winchester and Silchester respectively *(14)*. The last of these may have originally passed slightly to the north of London, which was probably not founded until a few years after AD 43; if so it should be thought of as the Silchester to Colchester road in its earliest phase, when it was probably the only one of the three in existence. Unless there was an earlier course for this road, which is unlikely in view of the topography, it must be probable that the bridge at Staines was first constructed very early in the Roman period, to provide the required crossing of the Thames. Excavations further downstream at Brentford in Middlesex have shown that the early road there was 6m wide and was soon replaced by another version, 12m in width, perhaps in conjunction with a diversion of the road further east so as to head more directly towards the newly established London.

The London to Chichester road (Stane Street), as we know it, only makes sense in terms of a crossing at London, and should probably therefore be regarded as part of a package that included the foundation of the city, the construction of a bridge across the Thames, and the making of the roads to serve it. If there was a London to Winchester road, it also would have been part of this package, or added to it at a later date. The Thames crossing at London required considerable work and careful engineering for a road to cross the marshy areas around Southwark *(18)*. Stane Street was set out to cross the Weald Clay at its widest point and this also suggests a date for its construction some time after the initial conquest phase, when arrangements were being made to establish the province and exploit its potential: the primary purpose of London. What dating evidence we have for the construction of this road in its northern half, for example from Southwark and Alfoldean (just over the border into Sussex), suggests a date around about AD 50, which matches the suggested date for the foundation of London. The part of the road between the Chichester area and Pulborough, south of the Weald, may have been built earlier, to link these two places. This would explain why it does not take a more direct route towards London in Sussex. In this early phase it is possible that there was a link from Chichester to Colchester by going north and then round the Weald Clay, perhaps via the settlement at Iping and then up to Staines.

The route of the London–Silchester road is reasonably well known, although there have been few excavations across it in Surrey. Long straight stretches north and west of the county boundary in the area of Caesar's Camp at Bracknell are known as The Devil's Highway. It is probable that the route is then preserved for a time by the line of the Surrey border as it heads towards Egham. There are some problems with the course but it is possible that the road ran more or less to the Thames before turning east along the line of the later Egham Causeway (which may have been a medieval re-use of an original raised road course in this riverside location) and continuing along to Staines, where it crossed at the bridge. The latter has not been securely located; it may have been set across the river between Egham Hythe and the land behind the Old Town Hall. The long straight stretch of the road as it comes west from Brentford is heading for this crossing point. On the other hand it has been argued that the road altered course near the west end of the town and headed for a crossing closer to the present bridge, via the church 'island' *(15)*.

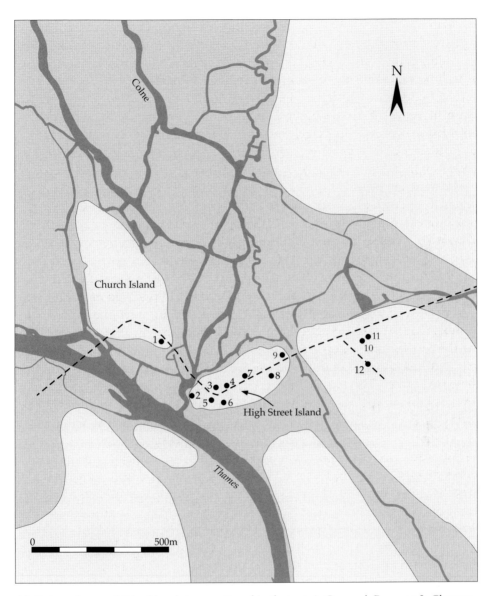

15 Staines: the gravel 'islands' and sites mentioned in the text. 1. Courage's Brewery; 2. Clarence Street; 3. 2-8 High Street; 4. Angel Inn; 5. County Sports (Market Place); 6. Johnson & Clark; 7. Tilly's Lane; 8. 73-75 High Street; 9. 78-88 High Street; 10. Old Police Station; 11. 18-32 London Road; 12. Kingston Road. *Drawing: Audrey Graham and author, after Jones 1982, fig 2*

The settlement at Staines itself grew up around the road which is more or less under the modern High Street, running along the middle of a slightly raised 'island' of gravel which helped to keep it above normal flood level. From Staines the route is well marked by the straight line of the old A30, designed to go as close as possible to the northern side of the Thames bend at Brentford. Official inns and horse-changing facilities were probably provided at Brentford, at Staines and at Wickham Bushes, near Bracknell.

Most of the London–Chichester road line has been known for a long time. The name Stane Street comes from Saxon words meaning 'stone road' and is applied to a number of Roman roads in England. As already noted, the line through the Weald is laid out in defiance of the subsoil and must have taken a great deal of hard work. It is not far from the scene of a description by William Cobbett on one of his famous 'rural rides' that well illustrates the difficulties of the terrain as late as 1823: '...From Ewhurst the first three miles was the deepest clay that I ever saw, to the best of my recollection. I was warned of the difficulty of getting along; but I was not to be frightened at the sound of clay. Wagons, too, had been dragged along the lanes by some means or another; and where a wagon-horse could go, my horse could go. It took me, however, a good hour and a half to get along these three miles. Now, mind, this is the real weald, where the clay is bottomless; where there is no stone of any sort underneath ...' (Woodcock 1967, 163). In Sussex the line is well preserved by the A29, an effect seen also in Surrey through the village of Ockley *(colour plate 1)*. North from there modern roads take a different route, but the Roman road has been traced in places such as Redlands Wood and North Holmwood.

The route through Dorking is not entirely clear, although current evidence suggests that the road may have passed close to the parish church before heading to the crossing of the Mole at Burford Bridge. From here the Mole Gap was avoided for a route over the Downs, starting with a steep climb from Juniper Hall up to Mickleham Downs, where a long straight stretch still survives as Pebble Lane, a public right of way that has something of the air the original road must have had. The road continued to Ewell, although its exact course in the Epsom area is still a matter for research. Its behaviour within the settlement at Ewell is of greater interest. The course from the north-east is known, still largely marked by the A24. The line in from the south-west has also been located, through excavation, but further excavation has failed to find the road on the logical line joining the two alignments. The evidence for Roman buildings in Ewell, which are likely to have lined the road, in fact suggests that the road took a double bend, not required by the topography *(23)*. It is possible that this was done in order to give prominence to a religious site, an idea that is discussed further below. North-east from Ewell the line of Stane Street can still be seen even from a glance at the Ordnance Survey 1:50,000 map, and it probably progressed more or less directly to Southwark, combining with Watling Street, the Canterbury–London road, not far south of the settlement *(18)*. It is sometimes suggested that Watling Street predates Stane Street and once headed to a crossing of the Thames near Westminster, but there is no evidence to support this theory.

Posting stations on Stane Street are known at Hardham and Alfoldean in Sussex, but the position of their equivalents in Surrey has caused debate, with no satisfactory answers as yet. Dorking and Ewell are the locations normally proposed, and there is no doubt that there were settlements at both places, each with a reasonable water supply (the Pipp Brook and the Hogsmill spring respectively). On the other hand, the usual distances between stations and their preference for a location at a river crossing might suggest that Burford Bridge and Merton are to be preferred. Posting stations seem to have been about 20-22km apart, which fits well enough with the Chichester to Hardham and Hardham to Alfoldean stretches. Alfoldean to Dorking would be a rather short stretch and a location at Burford Bridge would therefore suit better, with the Mole crossing and the place-name also in its favour. The *burh* element suggests a fortified place at the river crossing, which brings to mind the Roman-period earthwork enclosures known to have existed at both Hardham and Alfoldean, but at present no archaeological evidence is recorded for either enclosure or settlement at Burford Bridge. Whether the posting station was there or at Dorking, the distance to Ewell is too short. Against arguments that allowance is required for climbing onto the Downs it should be remembered that a similar climb (or descent) was required on the Chichester to Hardham stretch, which is of 'regulation' length. The area of the Wandle crossing at Merton has produced some evidence for Roman occupation in the form of pottery, building material and a large number of coins too spread in date and location to be a hoard. The location of Merton Priory might suggest a pre-existing Roman site, already 'developed' and useful for its materials. The distance to this site from Burford Bridge is not much over the expected length. Merton to London/Southwark is then only a relatively short stretch, but this is matched by the London to Brentford distance on the Silchester road, so it may be that a short first stage out from (or in to) the city was the norm. The posting stations were the official stops, but in all probability there were also inns at several other convenient locations, and the traveller chose according to his or her means and needs.

In contrast to the roads from Silchester and Chichester, the Winchester to London road is a problem. The rest of the road pattern all around London strongly suggests that such a road will have existed, and there is evidence for one heading in the right direction from Winchester most of the way to the Farnham area *(14)*. The fact that it gets this far, of course, supports the view that it must have gone on to London in some form. There are four main possibilities: a route to join the London road at Staines; a route towards a crossing north of Chertsey; a route to a crossing of the Wey near Burpham and then more or less along the line of the old A3; and finally a route also to a Wey crossing and then across to join Stane Street at Ewell. As yet, none of these routes have produced any evidence that can be regarded as convincing.

The Chertsey route may be marked for instance by a straight minor road line north-east from Chobham, with the possibly significant local place-name Stanners Hill, and such a road would help to explain the early post-Roman marking of Chertsey as an important place. If this road existed it would have continued north through Chertsey to cross the Thames and join the London–Staines road north of Ashford. On the other hand a road from Farnham along north of the Hogs Back would have gone near the Wanborough temples and then past several Roman sites in the north Guildford area to the Burpham crossing (where an old discovery of a few whole Roman pots indicates burials, and the place-name may indicate an enclosed settlement). From here it could take the old A3 line more or less to London. East of Ripley the local place-name Stratford Bridge could be a reference to a Roman road, although it is not recorded until relatively late. The route noticeably goes as close as possible to the bends of the Mole and the Thames in a way reminiscent of the London–Silchester road, while taking a more or less direct line, as would be usual.

Posting stations to match those on the other roads would then be expected, sited at appropriate river crossings if at all possible. A station is known at Neatham, near Alton in Hampshire, at the crossroads with the Chichester–Silchester road. If the road towards London from Neatham then continued more or less along the direct route and went to the north of the Hogs Back, the next posting station should be expected somewhere to the east of Farnham. The logical location beyond that, if the A3 route is taken, would be at the Mole crossing near Street Cobham. It is undoubtedly interesting that the mid point between Neatham and Cobham would then be in the vicinity of Wanborough, where evidence for Roman occupation is known some distance away from the temples. The distances would then be about the regular lengths. A posting station site adjacent to the Blackwater is perhaps rather more likely, because of the availability of a plentiful water supply, and it may be noted that recent excavations have located Roman settlement evidence at more or less the spot that would be predicted if the road took the suggested line and a location on or close to the Blackwater was required. The evidence suggests a higher status settlement and brings to mind a reference by Stukeley to a Roman site with stone buildings somewhere in the Tongham area. It would, however, be a long haul from the Blackwater to the Mole crossing.

There is some indication of Roman settlement on the west bank of the Mole near Cobham, marked by the Chatley Farm bath-house. This is usually interpreted as the surviving part of a villa, now lost to river erosion, but a bath-house would be equally at home in a posting station and there are several odd aspects about the site. The bath-house is late and has a far greater number of different examples of relief-patterned box tiles than any other rural site in Surrey; these patterns are also almost all unrepresented in the county except in Southwark, which with London is therefore the most likely source. The number of patterns suggests comparison with the sites at 15-23 Southwark Street and Winchester Palace in Southwark, both probably 'official' in some way. It may also be noted that petrological analysis suggests an Italian source for one tile fragment from the site, again perhaps suggesting a London source (possibly from material brought in as ballast). Chatley Farm is the nearest Roman site to Stoke D'Abernon church where two large dressed blocks of stone from a Roman building were recorded in the nineteenth century, suggesting an important nearby structure. All of these things suggest that the site had a high degree of 'pull' in the late Roman period, perhaps in keeping with an official role. If there ever was a posting station at Chatley Farm most of it must have been lost to erosion by the Mole, as recent fieldwalking failed to locate any extra evidence for buildings in the area. After the Mole the final posting station before London should be on the Hogsmill or the Beverley Brook. Nothing is known on the straight line crossings of the watercourses, but the possible settlement on Kingston Hill (see next chapter) would be reasonably well placed in terms of distance. Although not on a river crossing this site was probably well served by springs. There are of course far too many 'ifs' in this discussion and much more research will be needed before we can make suggestions about a London–Winchester road in Surrey with any degree of certainty.

As well as the main roads a number of other Roman roads have been located in Surrey, including two routes at the eastern end of the county, from London to the Lewes area and to the Brighton area respectively. Both may have served the Sussex ironworks in the Weald and perhaps also provided links to south coast ports. They will also have formalised some of the north–south routes used to exploit the resources of the Weald that had probably been in use for thousands of years before the Roman period. The line of the London–Brighton road is generally well established but the details of its course, particularly near London, are often still uncertain. It seems to have branched off Stane Street in the Kennington area and then run south through Streatham (another 'street' name) and Croydon to Godstone. South from here it ran over Tilburstow Hill to the course taken now by the A22 down to Blindley Heath from where the line down towards Sussex is less certain. The London–Lewes road branches from Watling Street not far from Southwark and then heads south to the line of the former Kent–Surrey border east of Croydon, a line followed to the top of the scarp slope of the Downs above Titsey where the road descends in a series of short straight sections terraced into the slope to the site of the Romano-Celtic temple. From here it headed south in a long straight section now cut by the M25 *(16)* before apparently deviating to the east across Limpsfield Chart and Crockham Hill and then rejoining the same straight alignment through Edenbridge and on towards Sussex, where the road is famous for its use of iron slag as metalling.

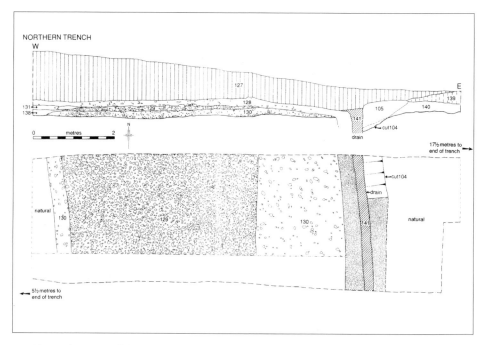

16 Plan and section of the London–Lewes road at the Clacket Lane service station on the M25. *From Hayman 1997, fig 3*

Several other roads may be suggested as probable. A branch from Stane Street is known heading north-west from the Alfoldean settlement in the direction of Farley Heath; its course from then on is still a matter for debate with one possibility a crossing of the Wey at Burpham and then a destination at Staines or Wickham Bushes on the London–Silchester road. There may also have been a Staines–Kingston road, perhaps with Ewell as the final destination, and Staines must have been linked by road with places to the north and west as well as to Silchester. It is also likely that there were routes along the lines taken by the later A246 and A25, north and south of the Downs. These may never have been metalled, but a Surrey greensand way to match the known Sussex equivalent is perhaps to be expected, following roughly the line of the A25. This is the appropriate point to note that the so-called Pilgrims' Way, also known as the North Downs Way, was probably never a through route of any importance. It is a romantic invention of the eighteenth and nineteenth centuries; the A25 route has much more to recommend it (including to any medieval pilgrims, as it is where they would have found both inns and churches).

In the Middle Ages, surveyors used highways to define the location of pieces of land; manorial courts fined people for misusing or failing to maintain the highway, which had definite boundaries and did not belong to the adjacent landholders. A similar system must have held good in Roman Britain, even for local roads, to judge by the writing tablet about Julius Bellicus' wood, quoted in the previous chapter. One boundary was defined as 'the vicinal road'. We do not know what this road was like, but it was obviously not a main highway. There were no doubt reasonably maintained tracks to most of the villas, especially where the subsoil was difficult, as at the Ashtead Common villa, where a metalled road branching from Stane Street was found *(43, 54)*. This would have been essential to allow the movement of heavy tiles across the London Clay. Other villa service tracks may not have required metalling as such.

We can only speculate about the use of the roads, for there is very little specific evidence. Britain was the home of chariot warfare, and many of the Latin words for vehicles are actually Celtic in origin, so we can reasonably expect a variety of wheeled vehicles like the ones shown on reliefs in other parts of the western empire. These may have included sleeping carriages for the well-to-do, and fast coaches for the official postal system, as well as wagons varying from heavy-duty carts to tanker wagons with huge barrels. A bronze linch pin found near Chelsham and a less elaborate one of iron from Stane Street near Cherkley Court are the only traces of these vehicles: we can only speculate about the effect of their loss.

Discussion of what was transported by road needs to take account of the likelihood of river transport, but this is unfortunately also a matter for speculation at present. The Thames was probably used, although the difficulties should not be underestimated. Goods may have been transferred to river-going craft in Southwark and the settlements at Staines, North Kingston and perhaps Putney may have played a part in trade up the river but there is little to show that this was the case. Transport on the Mole is sometimes postulated, but only by those who do not know the river, and on the Wey, with rather more justification. Malcom Lyne has demonstrated that it is possible to transport pottery from the Alice Holt/Farnham kilns to London by punt, but the Wey is now a very different river from the days before the making of the Wey Navigation in the mid seventeenth century. Even with the Navigation in place the nineteenth-century Farnham potter William Smith preferred road transport for his products and it is most likely that Roman pottery from the area was also transported by road. This must have been the case with tiles from places like Ashtead; indeed many tileries are sited in such a way that road transport is the only option *(17)*. As tileries could have been established in places with much better options for river transport we must conclude that it was not considered necessary.

Road transport must also have served to deliver produce from the farmed areas and from the villas and their estates to local markets and to London and Southwark, or to the army. We must postulate wagons of grain and animals driven in on the hoof. Timber and wood products must also have been constantly on the move, and some materials such as iron from the Wealden

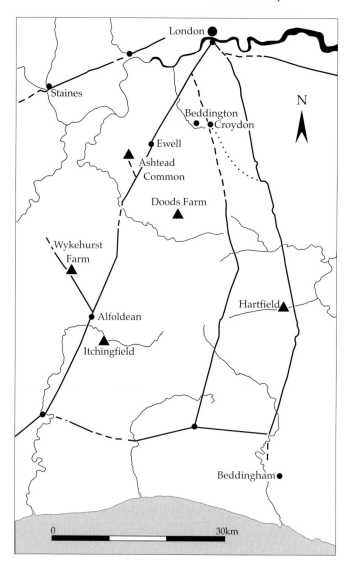

17 Location of tile kilns (triangles) in and near Surrey and their relationship to the Roman roads. Tiles produced at Hartfield (Sussex) are known to have reached both Beddington and Beddingham. *Drawing: Audrey Graham and author*

production centres travelling up to serve the industry in Southwark, and stone from the Reigate area. The roads may therefore have been busy, giving rise to a profitable passing trade which helped to foster roadside towns and villages, as well as opening up new areas to permanent settlement.

FIVE

TOWNS AND ROADSIDE SETTLEMENTS

In Surrey, towns as such were very much an introduction of the Roman period. But towns must have a function to support them and the proximity of London together with Surrey's low population up to the nineteenth century has meant that the county's towns were very small until then. It is not surprising therefore that there is little evidence for Roman towns in the area. Southwark, essentially of course part of London, was by far the largest settlement; Staines, with a similar origin and situation, was perhaps the next largest, big enough to be regarded as a 'small town'. Its importance as a Thames crossing point about midway between London and Silchester (and presumably with a link to Verulamium via the Colne valley) will have added to its basic function as a stopping place on the road, and its location on the Thames may also have been important. Of the others only Ewell has produced enough evidence for it to be clear that there was a nucleus of several buildings over an area large enough to warrant description as a town or large village. As we shall see, it may have had an extra function as a religious centre and this could have stimulated some extra growth. Development pressures have led to most recent archaeological work being carried out in Southwark and Staines, with a resulting increase in knowledge, but this of course will also have biased our understanding in comparison to other centres.

There are a number of other possible roadside settlements, identified in the previous chapter, which probably owed their existence to the passing trade and acted as market centres for the nearby farms or other activities in the countryside. Similar sites in other counties suggest that there was a ring of such settlements on the roads out from London, at about 15-20km distance. In each case the evidence is not very clear, generally no more than a combination of a scatter of Roman finds, including building material, and the location of the place. Flue-tiles found at Merton, Kingston, Croydon, and Dorking may hint at the former presence of bath-houses and therefore perhaps inns, but as there is clear evidence for tiles being reused for other purposes and sometimes even being taken to other sites, better evidence is needed to confirm the point. Patterns on some of the tiles from Ewell and Kingston indicate that they were probably Ashtead products, but there are examples from Croydon and Dorking not recorded elsewhere in the county. This suggests that they are more likely to have been originally delivered to these places as part of special orders connected with bath-house construction, rather than being reused building material.

This is not the place for a detailed description of Roman Southwark, which deserves a book to itself. A brief survey is, however, required because the settlement will have served as the de facto centre for much of Roman Surrey and it provides good local examples of some things difficult to illustrate in the other towns, although they will certainly have existed. Southwark was in fact in Surrey until the late nineteenth century: *Suthringa geweorche*, the earliest recorded form of the name, can be translated as 'the defensive work of the men of Surrey'. But Southwark's fortunes have always been closely bound up with those of London on the opposite bank of the Thames. Its location outside the jurisdiction of the city in the medieval period and later, meant that the settlement provided entertainments for Londoners that were not available or were more difficult to obtain on the north bank. It is often suggested that the same was true for the Roman period, but unfortunately the evidence is insufficient to justify such a conclusion. It is probably more correct to view the settlement as the southern version of similar informal expansion to the west along the roads out from the original planned London settlement. An inscription found recently in the Tabard Square development may imply that Southwark was simply seen and administered as part of the city *(85)*. It was dedicated by Tiberinius Celerianus who describes himself as *moritix Londiniensis*. *Moritix* is a Gaulish word meaning merchant (the Roman equivalent would have been *negotiator*).

A Roman mosaic was noted in Southwark as early as 1658. By the beginning of the twentieth century quite an impressive list of chance finds could be made, making it clear that there was a large Roman settlement. As the Second World War drew to a close it became clear that the many bomb-damaged sites would require redevelopment, and Surrey Archaeological Society took the lead in organising the evaluation of some of these sites. Work by Kathleen Kenyon between 1945 and 1947 established that important archaeological deposits survived, but it was not until the 1960s that rescue archaeology began in earnest and there have been large-scale excavations from the 1970s to the present day: at the time of writing the Tabard Square site is much in the news. Over the decades these excavations have made it increasingly possible to understand the topography long invisible under this built-up part of south London, and the extent of the Roman settlement.

Southwark came into existence as a result of the foundation of London, in about AD 50. The place chosen for the new city was at the lowest point on the Thames where it was convenient to bridge the river, and perhaps at the contemporary tidal head. The location had higher ground on the north bank to provide a suitable spot for a planned settlement and islands on the southern side of the river acting more or less as giant stepping stones for the course of the road *(18)*. The position echoes that of major trading places on the great rivers of Gaul which flourished in the Roman period, Bordeaux, Nantes and Rouen, and must have been a deliberate act of policy, with the aim of exploiting the new province. Stane Street was probably constructed as part of the overall plan and designed to join Watling Street just to the south of the island approach to the bridge; from here a single road was laid out across the islands (roughly along the line later taken by Borough High Street), often set on timber piles or corduroys to provide an adequate base. The original idea seems to have provided for a planned settlement on the north bank centred on the bridge, but growth was phenomenal and there was already extensive development beyond the formal grid by the time of Boudica, a matter of only about ten years. Southwark was part of this expansion, even though the site was not especially promising, being low lying and divided into separate islands, north and south. The pre-Boudican buildings so far recorded were found in remarkable excavations by the Museum of London Archaeological Service in advance of the construction of the Jubilee Line. They had been constructed along the road leading to the bridge on the drier part of the north island.

As we have seen, the early settlement was destroyed in the Boudican rebellion, but the site was soon cleared for rebuilding and over time much of the area of the two islands became built up. The watercourses were managed by revetting the channels. At its height, the settlement may have occupied more than 12ha (about 30 acres). There is no evidence for formal planning, but one second-century building with a portico fronting the main road on the north island has been interpreted as a *macellum*, or special market building. In general, buildings seem to have lined the main road and then expanded behind it as people chose. One well-maintained road is known heading south-west from the bridgehead; it has been suggested that it continued beyond the settlement but there is no evidence that it was more than an important internal road, perhaps only on the north island. Parts of more than 20 stone-founded buildings are known in Southwark, mostly on the north island, some with mosaics, tessellated floors and fine wall paintings. There is also evidence for more than 40 clay and timber buildings, more evenly divided between the two islands *(19)*. Unfortunately the evidence is rarely sufficient to provide much in

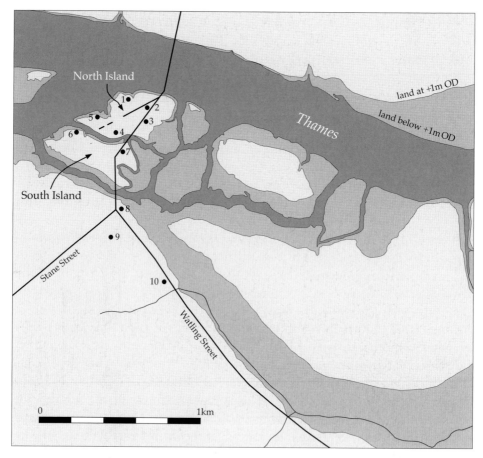

18 Southwark: the 'islands' and sites mentioned in the text. 1. Winchester Palace; 2. Southwark Cathedral; 3. Jubilee Line, Borough High Street; 4. 15-23 Southwark Street; 5. Courage's Brewery; 6. America Street; 7. 117-137 Borough High Street; 8. Tabard Square; 9. Swan Street; 10. Great Dover Street. *Drawing: Audrey Graham and author, after Sheldon 2000, fig 8.1*

the way of building plans, especially for the timber buildings. One exception on the Courage Brewery site, a wooden building dated by dendrochronology to about AD 152, had a remarkably well-preserved floor of oak. It measured about 4.75 by at least 11m and as it had a ramped (downward) entrance is assumed to be part of a warehouse.

The stone buildings include an extensive and high quality complex with baths and heated rooms on the site later occupied by the medieval Winchester Palace. Parts of the impressive painted wall decoration have been reconstructed from the scattered remains. The building was started before the mid second century and seems to have had some sort of military connection, to judge by the fragments of a large inscription recovered from the site, that gives lists of names grouped into cohorts. It may have served some sort of military guild.

19 Modern rescue archaeology: Borough High Street, Southwark. Part of a Roman clay and timber building can be seen in the foreground, and behind it post holes indicating further structures. *Courtesy Pre-Construct Archaeology*

20 Building with stone walls and tessellated floor, Tilly's Lane, Staines. *Courtesy Wessex Archaeology*

Another large building complex was found near Winchester Palace, at 15-23 Southwark Street. Its construction started earlier, around AD 75, and it had a long life, continuing into the third century. By the fourth century, however, the site was in use as a burial ground, which indicates a contraction in the settlement area. The building had rooms with tessellated floors and hypocausts round a courtyard and has been interpreted as a *mansio*, although other explanations are possible. The later buildings on the site have associated finds indicating particularly high status, such as glass tesserae from high quality mosaic floors or wall decoration, and marble from eastern Mediterranean sources, which suggests a private or official complex of higher status than a *mansio*.

It is likely enough that some of the buildings were inns, and others housed traders and craft specialists. There is plentiful evidence for iron smithing and copper alloy casting within the settlement, especially along the north–western fringe, apparently dating from the early Flavian period right up to the end of the fourth century. It has been suggested that this was mostly to provide for the needs of Southwark itself. Other evidence indicates that there was probably also horn, antler and leather working. The settlement has produced good evidence for widespread trade in particular with the western Empire, in which Tiberinius Celerianus no doubt played an active part *(85)*. If there were ever large wooden waterfront structures along the main course of the Thames, like those in London on the north bank, they will have been destroyed by later river action, but there is evidence for river boats within the island channels and for wooden structures from which they may have been loaded. It has now been shown that the islands near the settlement were used for agriculture and no doubt the watery environments were exploited in various ways. It is perhaps most likely that maximum use was made of potential meadowland and other grazing to provide for the needs of the animals used to supply motive power. Food for the human population could have been more easily brought in from farms further out, even many miles away, either by road or by water.

The settlement derived its water supply from wells, some of which have well-preserved timber linings (26). When they could no longer be used these were filled with a variety of material, often suggestive of a ritual of termination (71). This phenomenon together with other evidence for religion in Southwark is discussed in more detail in a later chapter, as is the evidence for burials. The main cemeteries seem to have been along Watling Street and Stane Street before they cross to the south island (18, 63). The recently discovered cemetery at America Street indicates that some parts of the south island at least may also have been outside the formal settlement area. Late burials within sites formerly used for buildings, as at 15-23 Southwark Street, suggest that the settlement area had begun to contract in the fourth century.

Evidence from some sites in Southwark, as in London, has been interpreted to mean that there was something of a decline in the town's fortunes in the third century, with a recovery in the fourth but with less dense settlement. Occupation levels are succeeded by a 'black earth' (or dark earth) which is taken by some to be indicative of abandonment or use for agriculture. Others consider that it may have been created by intensive use for low status buildings. There are probably different explanations for different sites, particularly as the black earth seems to start at different times. The pottery and coin evidence is complicated by questions of fluctuations in supply at certain times within the Roman world, which may cause dating problems for archaeologists. At present therefore this is an area of debate, with some seeing decline and decay while others argue that vigorous town life continued to the end of the Roman period. As late Roman London was defended by a very extensive wall circuit, had a functioning amphitheatre and crowded cemeteries, it must be likely that it had a large population. Southwark was apparently not defended, but its situation would have made this difficult and the view may have been taken that those who wished could take refuge in the city in times of danger.

Like Southwark, Staines grew up at a bridging point on a gravel 'island' in a generally wet area. It is situated at the confluence of the Thames and the Colne and a number of other watercourses that meander about the Colne valley (15). Beyond the rivers on both banks of the Thames are extensive gravel terraces with major prehistoric monuments such as the Neolithic causewayed camp at Yeoveney and the cursus near Stanwell. Staines is the only place in Surrey whose Roman name we know. *Pontibus*, 'at the bridges', could hardly make more obvious the origins of the town. The name is given in the document known as the Antonine Itinerary, which sets out a number of routes in Britain (and other parts of the Empire). It is unfortunate that the Stane Street route does not figure in the information that survives, as this would give us more names.

Apart from an occasional antiquarian reference to chance finds there was no archaeological work in Staines until the late 1960s. This was unfortunately no more than salvage work during redevelopment and there is no doubt that important archaeological evidence was lost with very little record. In particular, the Barclays Bank site is known to have had surviving evidence for a building, including plastered walls, and many objects, some of which were rescued (but with no proper archaeological context). From the 1970s more adequate rescue excavations could be arranged and these have continued to date, most recently with a large area on the north side of the town being examined, although mostly beyond the settlement area itself. As in Southwark, this work over thirty years or so has made it possible to gain much greater understanding of the Roman-period topography.

Reports on much of the archaeological work carried out in Staines are nearing publication. What follows is therefore based mostly on currently unpublished reports prepared by Rob Poulton and Phil Jones of the Surrey County Archaeological Unit and Jackie McKinley of Wessex Archaeology. Like Southwark, the area of the later Roman town in Staines has produced some evidence for prehistoric activity, but nothing to suggest anything more than agriculture as on other nearby sites. In the case of Staines, there is little sign of middle or late Iron Age activity at all. The town is also like Southwark in the sense that the settlement seems to have grown up along the road to the all-important bridge. There is no sign of formal planning or deliberate plantation. Staines was probably about a third the size of Southwark, and appears to have had only the one road with no evidence for side streets.

The earliest evidence for buildings in the town seems to be of the Neronian/Flavian period, that is from about AD 65-70. There are finds of earlier material which could perhaps be associated with road and bridge-building activities. Coins suggest a high level of activity by the later first century and there was rapid development along the road up to the end of the second century, when the settlement was probably at its height. Late first century and second century structures so far noted were of timber, although there is not much evidence for building plans. A possible round house was recorded on the Market Place site, apparently constructed as late as the end of the first century. It may have been set behind a more important building on the street frontage or even be associated with a possible ritual use of the site. There is evidence for buildings in the town with tessellated or *opus signinum* floors, hypocausts and tiled roofs by the early second century. *Opus signinum* is a kind of pink cement with crushed tile often associated with bath-houses.

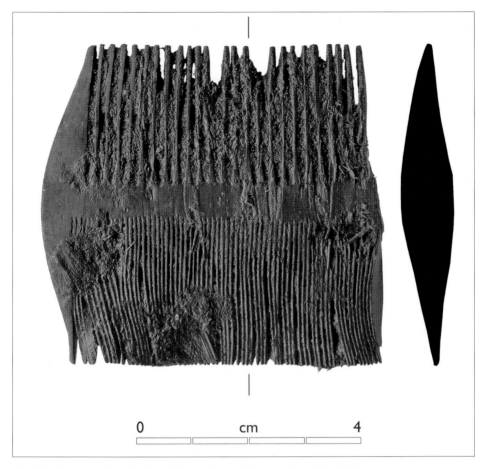

21 Wooden comb from Staines. *Courtesy Surrey County Archaeological Unit*

From the mid second century some buildings had stone foundations and there is evidence for painted plaster.

Traces of timber buildings have been found on a number of sites, such as Johnson & Clark, 73-75 High Street, Tilly's Lane and 78-88 High Street, although it has been suggested that there were fewer buildings north of the High Street, with at least some of the area given over to rubbish disposal. This may be simply a reflection of the fact that most archaeological investigations have been to the south of the High Street, as sites at 2-8 High Street and the Angel Inn site nearby have produced evidence for occupation and there are also findings of hypocaust-related material further east. The Tilly's Lane site also had a later second century stone-founded building with red tessellated floors surviving *in situ (20)*; it probably did not last long as the floors subsided into earlier pits used for rubbish disposal (by up to a metre in places!), and there may have been a fire, although there was time for the walls to be replastered and painted. The building had flint and rubble foundations and there was evidence that one of the rooms that did not survive had a mosaic. This indication of a higher status building is matched at the Johnson & Clark site, where there is evidence for the former existence of a black and white tessellated floor and a hypocaust. Earlier buildings on this site had been burnt down in the late first or early second centuries. There is also a nineteenth century record of a tessellated floor at the Angel Inn site, on the opposite side of High Street. Several sites in Staines have produced evidence for ovens, hearths and wells, some again showing evidence for ritual termination, as in Southwark and elsewhere.

Third-century Staines is difficult to assess; it seems that the town was always in danger of flooding but this may have reached the extent of leaving only a maximum 140m wide strip around the road in winter, perhaps even reaching right up to the road in bad years. Ditches were dug along the edges of the town as flood defences (they have been found for example in Clarence Street and Tilly's Lane). The serious third-century flooding was possibly the explanation for an apparent decline in the town's fortunes; although this is paralleled in Southwark and elsewhere it seems to be more marked and to begin earlier in Staines. At present it is not clear how well the town recovered from this decline; there is some evidence to suggest that the area became much more rural in the fourth century, with considerable use for animals and midden deposits. It may be that the settlement moved further to the east, especially as bad winter flooding continued into the early part of the century, although it seems to have got drier later on and there is evidence from plant remains indicating unusual flowering, probably to be associated with very hot summers. For what it is worth, coin evidence implies that activity continued at least to the end of the fourth century.

The coin use may indicate that town life of a sort continued to a greater extent than suggested. Evidence also shows little change in the diet of the town throughout the Roman period. Pits and other features continued to be dug in the fourth century and later Roman levels are inevitably more disturbed by development in later periods, and their evidence (particularly for shallower features) lost or damaged. The black earth noted in Southwark is also present on Staines sites, as for example at 2-8 and 73-75 High Street, but its meaning is still a matter for debate and it may imply occupation rather than abandonment. A few finds also suggest the possibility that there was activity in the town in the early post-Roman period.

Evidence for iron smithing and other metalworking, probably like Southwark for local use, has been recovered from a number of sites. Waterlogged deposits on the western fringes of the town, for example at Clarence Street and in the Riverside Gardens site near the Old Town Hall in the Market Place, have produced evidence for leather working, perhaps to be associated with previously noted evidence for the butchery of cattle. As well as

22 Staines: inhumation burial. *Courtesy Surrey County Archaeological Unit*

leather shoes and offcuts, finds included a rare wooden double-sided comb *(21)*, a timely reminder of the kind of common item that is usually missing from the archaeological record. Presumably rubbish was being thrown into the marshy foreshore areas; associated pottery suggests that the leather working took place at least in the second and fourth centuries. Rubbish disposal here supports the view that the Thames frontage was not used for installations for river trade; perhaps vessels were taken into the Colne mouth to 'dock'. Widespread trade is indicated by a good range of imported pottery and the town may have acted as a centre for the dispersal of high quality pottery produced locally; lead-glazed vessels (copying samian forms like the bowl illustrated on *64*) are thought to have been made somewhere nearby.

Evidence for activity in the Roman period has been found on gravel 'islands' near the town island. Across the Thames at Egham Hythe there are traces of occupation and at the Courage Brewery site on the church 'island' to the west there is Roman building material. It is not known if this was simply material taken outside the town to dump, or if it could indicate structures from a cemetery like the one at Great Dover Street in Southwark *(63)* or even be associated with a religious site. The later presence of the church on this island would not be without parallel in a former Roman cemetery area. On more 'islands' to the north, evidence from the Central Trading Estate indicates the existence of fields and enclosures, and has provided some information about the food produced and for the general environment of the town (see below). To east and south, along the London and Kingston Roads, Roman-period burials, both cremations and inhumations, have been found *(22)*. There is also evidence which has been interpreted as occupation here in the fourth century, which is unusual in a cemetery area. It may indicate expansion of the town, or possibly implies a radical shift in the settlement pattern as suggested above.

Ewell is the only other place in the area to have produced convincing evidence for a large Roman period settlement. Diamond's recording of the ritual shafts to the east of the village in the 1840s appears to be the first archaeological work to have been carried out. Chance finds were recorded from the settlement proper from the 1930s onwards, and there were various small-scale excavations from then up to the 1950s. Ewell has not been subjected to large-scale redevelopment and so archaeological rescue work from the 1960s has been relatively limited and until recently was carried out by the local society. Publication of the results has often been delayed because the directors have then moved away from the area, although better progress has been made in the last few years.

Excavations and chance finds show that there is evidence for occupation stretching more or less along the line of Stane Street for around one kilometre, probably centred around the Hogsmill spring, which has attracted human settlement since the Mesolithic (Middle Stone Age) *(23)*. As yet no convincing evidence has been found for any formal planning or the boundary of the settlement, whether defended or not. As we have seen, the course of the Roman road is not completely established through the village, but it is likely to have entered from the south about 100m to the east of the Epsom Road/High Street line and then turned along the line of Cheam Road towards the spring before turning again to pick up the line towards London. Over 400 coins are recorded from the area and together with pottery they indicate occupation throughout the Roman period. Most of the coins follow the general line of Stane Street, but a spread to the south-east perhaps hints at the presence of another road. There have also been claims of evidence for other roads from the west, which might suggest that the postulated London–Winchester road in fact crossed to combine with Stane Street at Ewell.

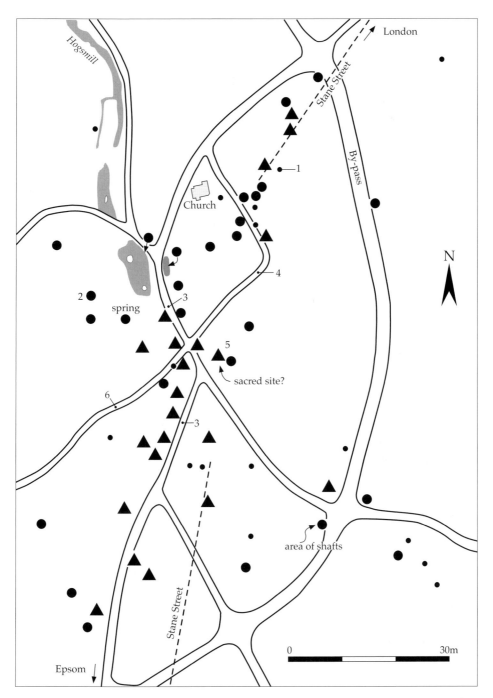

23 Ewell: area of occupation. Triangles are sites with building material; larger dots are sites with other features, pottery, etc; small dots are coins only. 1. Church Field; 2. Bourne Hall; 3. High Street; 4. Church Street (the original church stood within the angle in the road); 5. King William IV; 6. West Street. *Drawing: Audrey Graham and author, after Abdy and Bierton, 1997, map 1*

Several sites have produced building material including heating system tiles, but only two small parts of stone-founded buildings are known, from St Mary's Churchyard Number 4 (north-east of the church). Recent excavation in Church Field located the course of Stane Street together with evidence suggesting the presence of two buildings including a hypocaust and occupation from the first to the fourth centuries. More recently still, work by Oxford Archaeology at Glyn House found evidence for one or more timber buildings on a site in use from the late first to the end of the third century (*23*: site a little to the north of the Church Street/High Street junction). In particular there were two parallel lines of post holes probably indicating an aisled building. It seems to have had a cleared yard behind it whose opposite end was marked by a mass of pits, backfilled with rubbish. There were three probable wells. The suggested aisled building has a very rural air for a structure in the centre of a Roman town, even if it was set back from the street frontage and subsidiary to a more townlike road frontage building. It perhaps strengthens the feeling that Ewell was less a town than a straggling roadside village, albeit one that had a good standard of living to judge by the imported pottery (including from the Glyn House site itself). Sites in the High Street, Church Street and West Street have also produced some evidence for buildings, pits and a well and a notable chance find from the churchyard was a probably imported wine strainer with zoomorphic design.

It has recently been proposed that the site behind the King William IV public house near the village centre may have been part of a religious complex, possibly continuing a tradition from prehistory. The area around the Hogsmill spring is also likely to have been important in this context and there have been finds suggestive of votive offerings there. The shafts recorded by Diamond (*24*) are not far to the south-east and offerings similar to those found in the shafts are known from wells in the village and other nearby sites, which all adds to the general air of religious importance for the settlement as a whole. This aspect, explored in greater depth in a later chapter, may have been one reason for Ewell's importance in the Roman period. Another could have been to act as a centre for a local woollen industry. Animal bone evidence from the settlement indicates that sheep were overwintered and well cared for. Large flocks of sheep were kept nearby on the Downs in the Middle Ages. A Roman double ended iron wool comb is known from the settlement and like others from Britain is considered to be indicative of woollen production on a more than domestic scale.

In Dorking north of the High Street, sites in Church Street, around the parish church and in the adjacent newly-created Church Square have produced evidence for occupation throughout the Roman period, mostly in the shape of pottery and some building material, including a box flue-tile. The earliest recorded feature is a small ditch near the southern Church Street frontage dated towards the end of the first century. Later ditches have also been recorded

24 Ritual shafts at Ewell. *From Diamond 1847*

together with a few pits *(25)*. At the moment there is no evidence to suggest that occupation spread further down the slope to the Pipp Brook and negative evidence to suggest that it did not. It is difficult to characterise Dorking's Roman settlement; there is a natural tendency to assume that it was a small roadside settlement because it later became a town, but it is not yet even clear which route Stane Street took through the area. One interesting comparison would be with the large villa at Bignor in Sussex, as Dorking would be in a very similar location, near the main road in the valley at the foot of the Downs. The area of courtyards and buildings at Bignor is over 150 x 100m, and this does not include ditches defining the landscape beyond. Such an area would easily cover the main spread of evidence at Dorking. The relatively low number of Roman coins so far recorded from the town might then be significant, as this is in marked contrast to other possible roadside settlements. As a comparison, the extensive excavations at the Rapsley villa produced only eight coins. Clearly a great deal more evidence is needed before reasonable conclusions can be drawn.

It is also difficult to understand the evidence for settlement in central Croydon. The later town was located on the headwaters of the Wandle at the

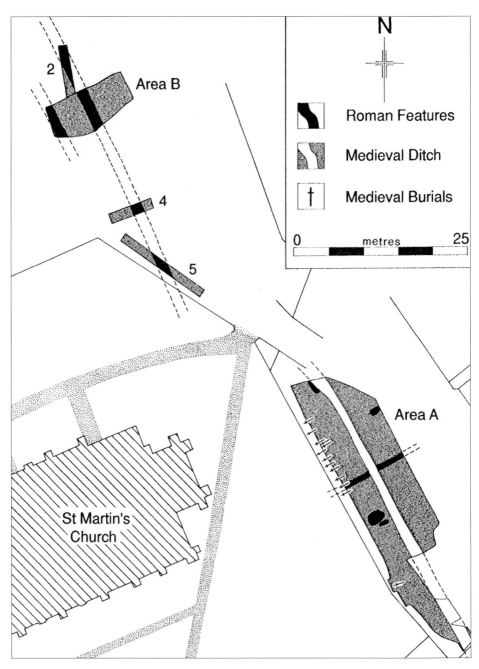

2

Area B

4

5

St Martin's
Church

Area A

25 Dorking: Roman ditches near the church. *From Hayman 1998, fig 3.2*

centre of an area of extensive prehistoric settlement. A general scatter of first to fourth century material is known from the area of the historic town including a large number of coins, some dated to the very end of the Roman period. Although occupation evidence is elusive early records indicate an extensive cemetery which suggests something more than a farm or villa. It is probable that much archaeological evidence has been lost to extensive redevelopment and even gravel digging, which occurred close to the High Street into the nineteenth century. Some finds were recorded by antiquaries when it took place. There has been recent archaeological excavation, as Croydon suffers from endless redevelopment, but this mostly shows only that sites are too disturbed to preserve archaeological evidence. Several Roman coin hoards have been found in the general area, although most are badly recorded (one apparently had nearly 4,000 fourth-century coins dating between AD 337 and 361).

Croydon's position near a source of the Wandle in the Roman period is a good one and was recognised as such both in the early Saxon period and by the Archbishops of Canterbury who made it an important residence. Evidence for farm sites is known in a number of places nearby for which Croydon would have made a logical market centre, and it may even have specialised in the production of the Autumnal Crocus (see further below). Charcoal burning for the London market could also have been an important local activity, as it was in later periods. It is probably safe to conclude that there was a roadside settlement at Croydon but it is to be hoped that better evidence will be found. The settlement was on the London–Lewes road, but the road has not been certainly located through the later town and its course has been postulated from the finds. If there was a roadside settlement then we would expect occupation sites lining it on each side, and there is little evidence for this, but the main scatter of coins does follow the old High Street line, a course which would have allowed the Roman road to follow the grain of the topography even if it meant something of a swing to the east of the direct line. As noted above, in Ewell the main coin spread is along the general line that Stane Street must take.

There is a small amount of evidence probably indicating Roman-period occupation in central Croydon, around Whitgift Street and Mint Walk, on opposite sides of the High Street. It is interesting that this is about halfway between the George Street and Edridge Road cemeteries, which ought to be outside their related settlement. A little further west, down the slope from the High Street ridge, there is other evidence suggestive of settlement around the parish church in the Old Town area. Limited excavation in this area has not, however, found actual evidence of occupation apart from unstratified pottery and building material. The latter includes fragments of box flue-tiles implying a nearby building with a hypocaust system, if not reused material. The total of 89 coins from the relatively small Whitgift Street excavation is rather high for an occupation site (although they do come from a period when coin loss is common). A closer parallel would be with the King William IV site in Ewell, suggesting a ritual site of some sort, which might explain the rather amorphous collection of pits and holes found on the Croydon site. This is supported by the presence of a pit containing a disarticulated but largely complete dog skeleton, because these are frequently found in ritual circumstances, and maybe also by a brooch and a silver ring. If the site was ritual it would fit with the increasing evidence for such sites at or near the centre of roadside villages.

There is good evidence for a cemetery in the area around the junction of George Street and North End and across to Park Street. Most of this evidence was found in the nineteenth century but some was recorded as far back as the mid-seventeenth century. It suggests an inhumation cemetery, with at least two lead coffins, indicating high-status burials. It would be reasonable to assume that the main cemetery was placed along the road to London from the settlement, so this tends to confirm the suggested road line along the High Street. Some other burials nearby may also be Roman, including a group in Surrey Street. This would have been outside the postulated settlement area to the west; there are records of pottery in the immediate area but it is unstratified and usually interpreted as indicative of fields. Recently a very late Roman burial has been located on the edge of the early Saxon cemetery in and around Edridge Road, south-east of the main evidence for Roman occupation. The cemetery is dated early enough in the Saxon period to suggest continuity of occupation from Roman times, an aspect explored in a later chapter.

Recent discoveries at Skerne Road to the north of Kingston town centre may indicate that evidence for a Roman-period settlement there has been mostly destroyed by river erosion, which would explain why residual Roman tile and pottery is found in alluvial deposits. The patterns of flooding and erosion associated with different branches of the Hogsmill are not yet fully understood. There are antiquarian records of an inhumation cemetery nearby, with associated finds suggesting that some at least of the burials were Roman, and as in Croydon this probably indicates a settlement larger than a farm or two. There are few finds from the town centre itself except a group from a former stream crossing in Eden Street which are almost certainly votive offerings (see further below). This is the place to note that a Roman altar sometimes said to be from Eden Street and described as though it was a local find was in fact first noted in the garden of a shop selling antiquities. It is likely to be an antiquarian import, being of a hard buff sandstone and and inscribed DEAE FORTUNAE ET NUMINIBVS AVGVSTORVM ('To the goddess Fortuna and the spirits of the Emperors'). These things together suggest a northern military bathhouse as the probable original location, from which the stone was removed to the south by a fashionable gentleman in the eighteenth or nineteenth century (like those used as features in Philip Carteret Webb's landscape garden at Busbridge near Godalming).

Antiquarian records also indicate the possibility of a settlement on Kingston Hill. Leland, writing in the sixteenth century, refers to frequent finds of wall foundations associated with Roman coins and 'painted' earthen pots, one of which seems to have contained a hoard of silver coins and perhaps other material, including silver chains. The site is certainly east of Kingston and somewhere near the main road over Kingston Hill. There are later references possibly to this site but also to what is probably a different site about a kilometre away to the south-east, at or near Coombe Nevill. Here there is also reference to foundations and a hypocaust and probably another coin hoard buried in a jar. The references are difficult to place accurately and some are repeating and perhaps embellishing earlier accounts. It is just possible that all refer to the same site.

On balance, it is likely that there was a substantial settlement somewhere near the road on Kingston Hill, with stone-founded buildings and an associated cremation cemetery, and a second site nearby, perhaps just a hoard of coins but also possibly a building with a hypocaust. Both sites could have been served by springs as they are near the locations chosen for Cardinal Wolsey's conduit houses, which gathered water to be piped down the hill and across the Thames for his great palace at Hampton Court. Guesswork might suggest a roadside settlement on Kingston Hill and a villa nearby at Coombe Nevill, but there could equally be a single important religious site and perhaps nearby burials and coin hoards. The picture is further complicated by the undoubted presence of a Bronze Age settlement in the general area, which may account for some of the reports of 'Roman' urns.

This brief survey will have shown that there is little sign of formal planning in the larger settlements of Roman Surrey, nor can we say much about the layout of buildings except in Southwark. These places must have had some kind of organisation and a place to gather so in each case there was probably some sort of central open space, possibly associated with a religious enclosure. If there were public bath-houses these too would have served as places to gather and discuss events. Any town that considered itself civilised should have had such a bath-house but although we have evidence for buildings with hypocausts it is not enough to be certain of their functions. Bath-houses gathered other aspects of town life around them, such as barbers and scribes.

It is unfortunate that buildings have been hard to find unless they were built of stone, which is always likely to have been the exception. Even the stone buildings are usually greatly disturbed by later building activity and by stone robbing. Hearths, areas of flooring and roof tiles indicate the presence of timber buildings but the difficulty in finding much evidence for their plans suggests that they were constructed using box-framed walls more or less laid directly on the ground and so leaving little archaeological trace. Occasionally they may be defined by the stumps of clay walls, perhaps surviving only because they were plastered *(19)*. The possible aisled building at Glyn House in Ewell is marked only by its aisle posts, with no trace of the outer walls, and this can also be seen in two ' barns' at the Beddington villa, suggesting that the

26 Roman well, 117-137 Borough High Street, Southwark. *Courtesy Pre-Construct Archaeology*

same building technique was in use throughout the area, both in towns and on rural sites. The Southwark 'warehouse' is an indication of what has been lost as a result; it would have left little archaeological evidence if it had not been waterlogged so that the wood survived. The characteristic building of Roman towns in Britain is the so-called 'strip house', that is a building with a narrow street frontage having a shop (often a workshop) in front and living accommodation behind. There is very little evidence that this was the case in Surrey, except in places along the main road on the north island in Southwark. It might be expected at least in Staines, but Roman street frontage plots there have not often been examined. As noted above, the settlement at Ewell may not have been very like a town and so these buildings are less likely to have existed there.

No-one in the towns will have been far from the countryside and the smaller places will have been more like large farming villages with the surrounding countryside worked from the settlement. There is evidence from Staines for the natural vegetation round the town: alder in the wetlands between the 'islands', holly, hawthorn, blackthorn, hazel and heather on drier ground; trees included willow, poplar, oak, birch, elm, beech. It is reasonable to assume that some of these continued to grow within the town itself. Hay was gathered locally for winter fodder for animals which would also have been grazed in the nearby fields and meadows. It is likely that this would have been particularly for oxen and mules, the primary motive power.

There is reasonable evidence for what was eaten and drunk in some of the settlements. Water came from wells *(26)* and amphorae show that some people could also drink wine. Beer was presumably also available. In Britain as a whole it is possible to see that towns and villas show a more 'Roman' diet, favouring beef and pork while mutton prevailed in the countryside continuing the Iron Age tradition. The use of the mixing bowl known as the mortarium (which had built-in grits for grinding) is also an indicator of Roman dietary habits, and more could be done by studying the distribution of these vessels. Different types of amphorae indicate the import of olive oil, important for cooking, lighting, cosmetics and medicines, as well as wine. They were also used for other products, such as the fish sauce known as *garum*, but as they could be reused as containers, interpretation of their presence on a particular site must always be tempered with caution. Evidence from Staines and Ewell tends to show this more-Roman diet but it is not yet adequate elsewhere for conclusions to be drawn. There is a hint from some sites in Ewell that mutton was favoured more than would be normal for a Roman town, but much more work is needed on animal remains from the settlement for this to be confirmed. Most of the food for towns must have been supplied from local farms but fruit and vegetables were probably grown, and pigs and fowl reared, in the settlements themselves. There is little sign that hunting provided much of the food. Domestic animals were usually driven in to be killed and butchered in town.

As well as the usual Roman town diet favouring beef, with some pork and mutton, Southwark has evidence for fig, walnut, grape, olive, raspberry, black-berry, mulberry, plum, peach, cherry, damson, apple or pear, lentils, peas, the cabbage family, coriander, mustard, dill, and cucumber. The delightfully named gold of pleasure may have been used to get oil from its seeds or may have been brought in as a weed among flax. The latter, together with hemp, was used to produce fibres for rope, hessian and linen. Olives and probably figs, peaches and lentils were imported, but the rest could have been locally produced. Staines has evidence for bread wheat, barley, emmer wheat, rye and oats (if not a weed), peas and field beans being cultivated. Wild plant foods were used throughout the Roman period: bramble, dog rose, sloe, wild plum, elder. There were also seeds from figs, strawberries, elderberries, sloes, cherries, and plums. Late on there is evidence for deliberately cut black mustard presumably to be used as a spice. In general there is little sign that the diet changed through time. As well as beef with some pork and mutton, there is evidence for duck, widgeon and goose. Ewell also had goose, with chicken, domestic dove, mallard and probably woodcock. In keeping with its more rural character it also had red and roe deer, and hare as well as beef, mutton and pork. Also present were horse, dogs from very young to old, one or two cats, weasel, hedgehog, house mouse and black rat, raven, crow and jackdaw. As with most Roman sites there were oysters, with mussels, and some cockles, whelks and winkles. Finds like these indicate the presence of an organised industry and trading network of which there is little other trace.

It is likely that many industries developed to serve the markets provided by the towns, and through them the countryside around them. The towns themselves also acted as production centres and provided a home for some specialist services. There will for example have been craftsmen producing metalwork such as fine enamelled brooches *(colour plate 7)*. Others will have made use of the plentiful material available from animal remains, producing leather goods, as in Staines and Southwark, and bone artefacts such as hairpins, handles and hinges. The serious lack of surviving organic evidence makes it very difficult to do more than guess at some of the material that must have been supplied and so attention is usually focussed on pottery and tiles in considering trade. For instance some pottery vessels probably served as containers for products such as salt and honey. Another aspect rarely visible in the archaeological record is the woodland industry which is considered in the next chapter. It must have been of huge importance for buildings and other structures, fuel (for home, bath-houses, industry), transport (carts and carriages, barrels, boxes) and many domestic objects, tools, fixtures and fittings *(21)*. The same is true for such things as basketwork (perhaps even being used for furniture) and flowers for garlands and scent (we know they were used much as we would use them today in other parts of the Empire).

The towns provided important markets for local producers of tiles and pottery, often from surprising distances, especially later in the Roman period. They were also probably the route by which imported pottery and other products such as glass reached the countryside (and as such hint at the route for other expensive products such as spices that have left no archaeological trace). Imports included samian ware from Gaul *(64)* and fine colour-coated vessels (such as the vessel decorated with a hunting scene found at Titsey (XII on *colour plate 16*), which is probably from the Cologne area. The special glass vessel from Rapsley has already been noted but the site also had several other more ordinary glass vessels which are likely to have been imported *(12)*, as were glass vessels in Staines *(65)*. The bulk of Surrey's pottery for everyday use came from the Alice Holt/Farnham industry but fine wares were usually obtained from elsewhere; later in the Roman period this was often from the Oxfordshire potteries, which had developed a samian substitute (for example I and XI on *colour plate 15*).

A very unusual find from Staines may bring this survey of the larger settlements to a close. It provides us with all too rare evidence for a specialist service available in a town: a healer or doctor. A *collyrium* stamp (often called an oculist's stamp) was found at the 73-75 High Street site in a fourth century pit *(27)*. It may by then have been regarded as having some talismanic properties and been deliberately deposited as an offering. The stamp is small and an

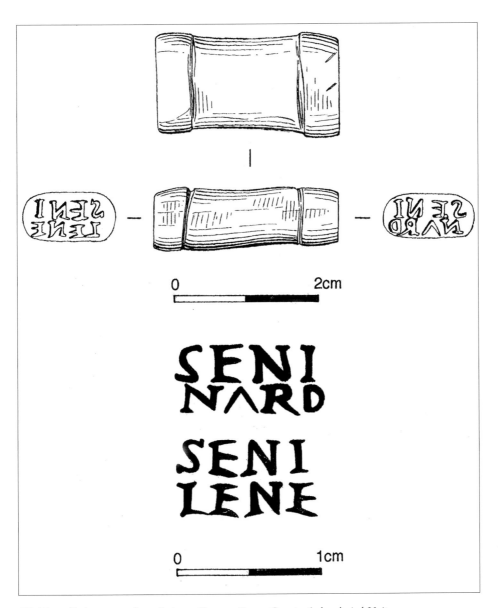

27 The *collyrium* stamp from Staines. *Courtesy Surrey County Archaeological Unit*

unusual shape and may have been cut down. Lettering is cut at each end for impressing into ointment. It is cut retrograde so that it comes out the right way round when impressed: SENI NARD and SENI LENE. SENI is a shortened form of a name. There are a number of possibilities, including Senicianus or Senius, but the expert Ralph Jackson favours Senior and wonders if he could be the same man as is attested at Kenchester near Hereford. NARD is short for *collyrium nardinum*, an eye ointment made from an aromatic resin called *nardum* mixed up with other materials including myrrh. LENE is for *lene-mentum* (or *lenimentum*), indicating a soothing remedy, again probably for eyes. These stamps are not common finds and this is the only one known from the south-east outside London. Jackson suggests that it implies the presence of a healer probably serving quite a wide area. He may have had colleagues or assistants: the Tilly's Lane site produced some bronze double-ended scoops, most often thought to have a medical use, including in connection with ointments. Another nearby Staines site has produced part of a scalpel and some of the environmental evidence from the town suggests plants gathered or grown for medicinal purposes. Perhaps part of Staines' earlier economic success was based on a steady stream of people seeking medical assistance and lodging in the town.

SIX

LANDSCAPE AND
SETTLEMENT

It needs a very large leap of the imagination to visualise what the Surrey countryside may have been like in the Roman period. We are not helped by the losses
of wildlife and wild plants in the period since the Second World War as a result
of our inability to control the huge forces for destruction (chemical and
mechanical) now at our disposal. Imagination is needed because our actual
knowledge of the Roman landscape is limited at the moment. What follows is
therefore speculative, but it serves to raise a number of interesting questions
that will hopefully lead to further research. A useful starting point is the
county's geology and topography.

Surrey is a small compact county, not designed by nature to support a large
human population. The geology is complex and therefore soils vary greatly,
sometimes even within the same field. They are often poor or difficult to work.
The land utilisation map published by L. Dudley Stamp and E.C. Willats in
1942 is shown here *(28)* as a more meaningful guide to the soils than geology
alone. The county lies on the northern edge of the Weald, and as a general
rule the subsoil deposits run east–west. Weald Clay is found along most of the
southern edge of the county (the Wealden Clay Plain), with a small area of
Tunbridge Wells Sand forming high ground in the extreme South-East
(Wealden Sand Ridges). The Clay curves round the great oval of the Weald
and is therefore not present on the very western edge of Surrey. It is very heavy
and in general is not suited to earlier forms of agriculture, although it is not
uniform and there are localised patches of more easily-worked material, particularly where the River Mole cuts through towards Gatwick.

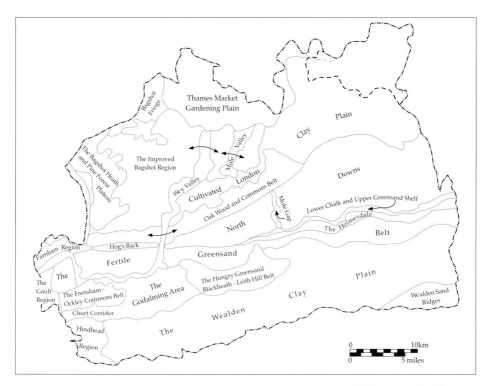

28 Land-use regions of Surrey in the early 1940s. The dashed area in the north-east corner was excluded as being within London County Council and heavily built-up. *Drawing: Audrey Graham, after Stamp and Willatts 1942, fig 22*

Labels within the map:

Bagshot Fringe

Thames Market Gardening Plain

The Bagshot Heath and Pine Forest Plateau

The Improved Bagshot Region

Mole Valley

Clay

Plain

Wey Valley

London

Cultivated

Oak Wood and Commons Belt

Downs

Mole Gap

Lower Chalk and Upper Greensand Shelf

Farnham Region

Hog's Back

North

The Holmesdale

Belt

Fertile

Greensand

The Hungry Greensand Blackheath - Leith Hill Belt

Plain

The Gault Region

The Frensham - Ockley Commons Belt

The Godalming Area

Clay

Wealden Sand Ridges

Churt Corridor

Hindhead Region

The

Wealden

0   10km

0   5 miles

29 Aerial view of the surroundings of the Wanborough temples. *Photograph: David Williams*

North of the Weald Clay is the Lower Greensand, particularly extensive in the south-west, because of the way it in turn curves round the Weald. Here it forms a kind of much-eroded plateau, the Greensand hills (Frensham–Godalming area–Hungry Greensand), which include the highest ground in the south-east and give rise to a scarp slope overlooking the Wealden plain. There are a number of different beds recognised in the Greensand, most of which give rise to soils so poor that they have traditionally been used as heathland. Across the northern edge of the deposit in the valley south of the Downs the soils are generally much better (The Fertile Greensand Belt), perhaps as a result of admixture from the Gault Clay and the Chalk. In the west of the county the early nineteenth-century writer Cobbett was favourably impressed by the corridor of richer soils around Churt, while regarding much of the rest of the Greensand as very poor indeed.

North of the Lower Greensand are thin strips first of Gault Clay, more extensive in the east (Holmesdale) and extreme west, around Farnham (The Gault Region), and then of Upper Greensand. These both outcrop along the southern edge of the North Downs, the steep scarp face. The Downs are formed of the remnants of the great chalk dome that once covered the Weald, with the other deposits already named forming successive layers beneath it: in descending order Chalk, Upper Greensand, Gault Clay, Lower Greensand, Weald Clay, Tunbridge Wells Sand. Erosion has, as it were, sliced the top off this dome, exposing the different layers in their turn. The northern side of the dome is represented by the dip slope of the Downs, falling comparatively gently down towards the north, while along the southern edge of the Downs erosion has removed the Chalk altogether, leaving a steep scarp slope. The pattern is of course repeated in reverse in Sussex. Rain percolates through the permeable Chalk until it meets less permeable layers, and this gives rise to springs both north and south.

Although the Downs are essentially composed of Chalk, it is misleading to think of them in this way in Surrey, because there are extensive superficial deposits of other materials, probably as a result of glacial action in the last Ice Age. Where the Chalk is exposed it produces relatively thin soils, which in places have certainly been used for agriculture but are perhaps more usually suited to grazing. The superficial deposits include the Clay with Flints, which is very extensive east of the Mole Gap. The resulting soils were usually regarded as only really suitable for trees even earlier in the twentieth century, but they vary locally and may also have been altered by use. For example, in the area around Walton on the Hill there seems to be some extra admixture which made the soils more attractive in the prehistoric and Roman periods, as the group of villas in this area suggests. There may have been a surface covering of a loess soil, whose loss in due course to erosion caused by overuse produced Walton and Headley Heaths, the name of the latter ('heath clearing') indicating that heathland here existed at least by the Saxon period. There are also other surface deposits on the Downs whose soils have given rise to heathland, not a land-use type normally associated with chalk.

To the north of the Chalk are the deposits of the London Basin, primarily London Clay overlain by extensive surface deposits in places. Immediately north of the Downs is a generally narrow strip of Thanet Sand, which gives rise to a light fertile soil, rarely of any great extent although more important in the east. The Clay itself is generally heavy, and of a character that historically has given rise to many wooded commons (Oak Wood and Commons Belt, *29*), although much has been cultivated in more recent times (Cultivated London Clay Plain). It is locally altered by alluvial deposits associated with the Wey, the Mole and the Wandle, together with the streams that serve them. Where these rivers approach the Thames and along that river itself there are large spreads of river gravels, especially around Staines and Chertsey and down towards Weybridge (Thames Market Gardening Plain) and around Beddington and Croydon. In general these deposits have been attractive to earlier agricultural activity and are well-known for archaeological discoveries. There are also older terraces of the Thames, preserved at a higher level, which are much less fertile, and sometimes form hills in the north of Surrey. In the north-west of the county there are large areas of Bagshot, Bracklesham and Barton Beds, a mixture of sands and clays which generally produce very poor soils and have traditionally been heathland. Some parts of this area (Improved Bagshot Region) have been used particularly for nurseries (of great national significance) over the last 200 years.

Writers in the eighteenth and nineteenth centuries vied with one another to express just how bad they considered the heathland of west Surrey, often suggesting that it was the worst in the country. Stevenson noted that 'it is difficult to conceive of a character of soil worse than that of the heaths of Surrey'. Cobbett described the area around Bagshot as 'the miserable heaths of Hounslow, Bagshot and Windsor Forest'. Defoe called Bagshot Heath a 'Black Desert', the land 'almost as bad as that between Godalming and Petersfield' on the Portsmouth Road. This is the area around Hindhead (currently England's second worst travel bottleneck) which Cobbett famously called 'certainly the most villainous spot that God ever made'. Marshall, who had extensive knowledge of Britain as a whole, said that the Surrey heaths were 'worthless, and in their present [late eighteenth century] state the most unprofitable to the community, of any district of equal extent, in the island; the mountains on the north-west coast of Scotland, perhaps, excepted'. Paradoxically, this has resulted in one of the glories of modern Surrey, the large surviving areas of open-access countryside.

The complex geology has given rise to a varied topography that in general terms can be seen as divided by the long chalk ridge of the North Downs running east–west across the middle of the county, very narrow west of Guildford where it is known as the Hog's Back. Major gaps have been cut through the Chalk by the Wey and the Mole, and are of course used by the main routes. Elsewhere roads and tracks are forced to climb across the barrier. To the north of this there are the lower-lying gravel terraces and the spread of London Clay, with local hills of other materials. To the south of the Downs there is in general a valley, especially between Shalford and Wotton (the Tillingbourne Valley), both sides of Dorking (the valleys of the Pipp Brook and the Mole) and east from Reigate (Holmesdale). South again are the hills of the Greensand plateau, much more marked in west Surrey, and reaching heights greater than the Downs, a fact consistently missed by the writers of guide books. Then south of that is the low-lying Weald Clay, stretching away towards the South Downs. North–south routes have often been forced to climb across the Greensand Hills and then the Downs, forming deep holloways in the process, especially on the sandy subsoils.

It has become rather unfashionable to assume that different subsoils will have a marked effect on human settlement, but in fact all our evidence suggests that this was the case, in Surrey at least. The fertility of soils and the ways in which they can be worked depend on subsoil deposits modified by circumstances: natural admixtures, aspect, water supply, climate, overuse. At present we cannot say much about the climate of our area in the Roman period, although, as has been noted, evidence from Staines suggests that it may have been hotter than usual in some of the fourth-century summers. This is a reminder that we should not assume that the climate then was exactly as it is today and, as we know from discussions of the likely effects of global warming, only relatively minor changes can affect what is grown.

Soils can be altered by deliberate human agency and this may have happened in Surrey in Roman times. The Elder Pliny notes the use in Britain of *creta argentaria* dug from pits and spread on fields to make them more fertile. It is likely that this material was chalk, and Roman period chalk pits are known at Ashtead, West Clandon and Farleigh. There may even be a link with the place-name Merrow, which Professor Richard Coates has suggested is derived from a British word meaning 'marl-place'. Cultivated land could also be fertilised by the spreading of 'night soil', or folding domestic animals on fields overnight. There is little real evidence for this, except perhaps for small amounts of abraded pottery found scattered over modern fields, which could represent the spreading of farmyard and other rubbish heaps. Soils can also be overused; in Surrey it is generally accepted that the heathlands were created as a result of agriculture on subsoils not able to take it. Although this probably usually happened in the Bronze Age, the presence of Roman buildings in certain areas such as Walton Heath and Puttenham Common suggests that some of the heathland may be a Roman-period creation. It should be stressed that eventually heathlands become tree-covered unless they are maintained by grazing, cutting or burning, as modern experience shows, and it is likely that some at least were so used in the Roman period. At the opposite extreme, some Surrey soils were still considered too heavy for agricultural use even in the early twentieth century, so it is reasonable to conclude that these have almost always been woodland.

In general, evidence for occupation sites suggests that the better, drier soils were favoured, as would be expected. Discussion of typical rural settlements is however severely hampered by lack of evidence for buildings, except for the villas. Even where there has been larger-scale excavation on rural sites, house plans have not been found. Thus an excavation at Atwood near Caterham produced clear evidence, in the form of post-holes, pits and ditches with associated pottery, for a Roman-period settlement site, but no recoverable building plans. At Thorpe Lea Nurseries the location of the settlement in its enclosure within a wider landscape can be seen *(30)*, but again no buildings. Even on the villa sites we can sometimes see parallel lines of posts suggesting aisled buildings, as at Beddington *(45)*, but no outer walls. At least here the walls can be assumed with a fair degree of certainty. It is likely that many rural sites continued to have round houses as in the Iron Age *(9)* until well into the Roman period. They may eventually have been replaced by rectangular buildings using the box-frame tradition that it has been suggested was in use

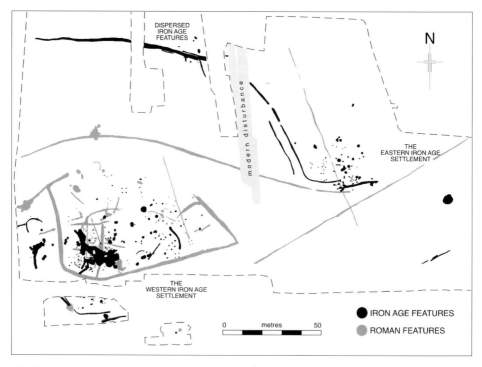

30 Thorpe Lea Nurseries, Iron Age and Roman-period settlement. Note the thin straight ditches, which probably mark a later Roman reorganisation of the landscape. *Courtesy Surrey County Archaeological Unit*

in the towns. Possibly the small early building at Rapsley (*36*, Period II) is a reasonably typical model for such structures, the evidence surviving here, where it does not on other sites, because the beams had been burnt and the evidence was then buried beneath substantial later buildings.

Throughout the western Empire villas are seen as a characteristic feature of the countryside in the Roman period, although as we shall see they may only be characteristic of certain kinds of countryside. The meaning of the term 'villa' is much discussed in academic circles but it is probably a rather sterile debate, like trying to define the meaning of 'village'. In practice most people understand well enough what is meant. It is reasonable to assume that the bulk of the population of Roman Surrey lived in the countryside, and that villas were the exception, but the lack of evidence for other structures makes it difficult to assess what non-villa settlement was like, or how it related to the villas. The lack of well-studied rural sites, and their associated cemeteries, also makes it difficult to assess the size of the population, or how it fluctuated through time. A considerable workforce would have been required to manage and work the land and provide for its own needs and those of the population of the towns and larger settlements. We have a little information that may help to provide an informed guess at the likely size of the Roman period population, but it cannot be much more than guesswork.

The population of Surrey in 1811 was nearly 324,000. This was of course the historic county, and over 200,000 of these people were living in the Borough of Southwark or the Brixton Hundred, that is, the area closest to London. The population was also noticeably more dense around Croydon, again no doubt because of the London factor. By contrast there were fewer than 3,000 in the Borough of Guildford. If we remove the London factor we are perhaps looking at 100,000 for our area. Guildford probably had a population of somewhat less than 1,000 at the time of the Domesday Book (the calculation can only be approximate as it involves an unknown multiplication factor for household size, among other variables). Using this ratio we arrive at a Domesday population for Surrey of around 30,000. Other calculations for Domesday-period Surrey would suggest that about 20,000 was a more likely figure. It has been calculated that London's population around 1100 was about 20,000, which is at the lower end of the total suggested for the height of the Roman period (20,000–30,000). Perhaps therefore Surrey's Roman population was at about the same level as at the time of Domesday, and somewhere in the range 20,000-30,000 might be a reasonable guess for the height of the Roman period, especially bearing in mind the need to make some allowance for the addition of the area around Staines.

If we knew with any degree of certainty the total number of villas in the county, and if we had a likely ratio for the number of villas to the overall size of the population, then a more accurate figure might be suggested, but such things are but dreams at present, and may always be so. It is possible, however,

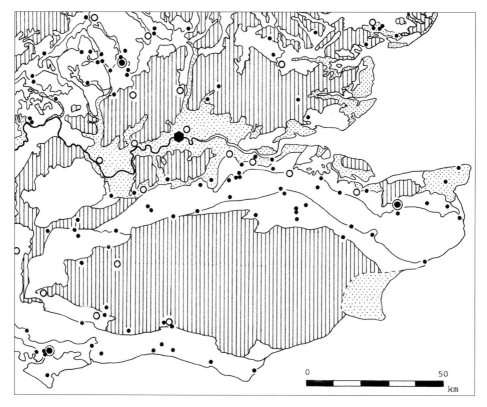

31 Distribution of villas (small dots) in the South-East. Open circles are small towns or roadside settlements; large circles with a central dot are major towns; the hexagon is London/Southwark. Major geological boundaries are shown; slowly permeable, mostly clay soils are indicated by vertical lines, and alluvium, sands and gravels are marked by dots. *Drawing: author, after Bird 2000, fig 9.3*

to examine the distribution of the known villas as a means of understanding the landscape better. Villas are comparatively easy to find and recognise, and therefore their known distribution may be more meaningful than that of other types of rural settlement. It is somewhat safer to argue that absence from certain areas is true absence and not simply a failure to find the evidence. When the distribution of villas in the South-East as a whole is examined it can be seen that it is the geology, or what arises from it, that is the key factor *(31)*. There is little sign that villas were simply grouped around towns, although such a relationship between the two is often claimed in the general literature. Modern writers still express surprise that there are not more villas close to London, or produce elaborate theories about the city itself to explain their absence, but an explanation based on the geology and on the use of the related soils is the most likely to be correct.

The evidence for Surrey villas is discussed in more detail below; what concerns us here is the location of known or likely sites. The first point of interest is that there is very little to suggest villas on the main river gravel terraces. The nearest possibility to Staines is an early record 'at Bakeham House' somewhere to the west of Egham and just beyond the gravels; Beddington and Carshalton are on the southern edge of the Wandle gravels and should more probably be seen as taking advantage of the Thanet Sand in this area. If the site on Kingston Hill is a villa rather than a larger settlement, then it may be noted that it is also away from the main gravels area. As might be expected there is little sign of villas on the Bagshot Beds except perhaps for the site at Lightwater.

In general terms the spring line north of the Downs might have been expected to attract villas, but there is little sign that it did so. Carshalton and the building near Ashtead church might be seen in this light, together with a little evidence in East Clandon (although the site is out onto the London Clay) and another hint at Wanborough Manor west of Guildford, but it can be seen that this is not a very convincing body of evidence. The East Clandon site is more reminiscent of the location of the Broadstreet Common/Barnwood villa, on the Clay north of Guildford; and the Ashtead Common villa is also on the London Clay. Sites on the Downs seem to be confined to the area east of the Mole. They include the villa at Chelsham *(32)*, early references that might suggest villas at Woodcote and Banstead, and the group of three villas at Headley, Walton on the Hill, and Walton Heath. Unfortunately none of these sites has produced sufficient evidence to indicate the reason for the choice of location, but presumably it included access to areas of chalk downland and some use of the Clay with Flints.

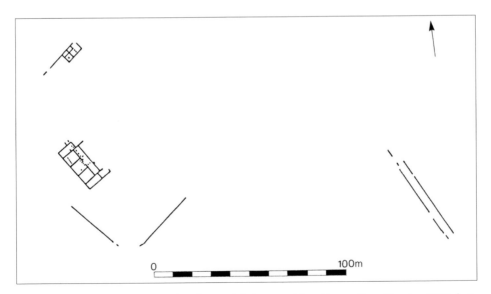

32 Plan of the villa at Chelsham, based on aerial photographic evidence. *From Hampton 1996, fig 1*

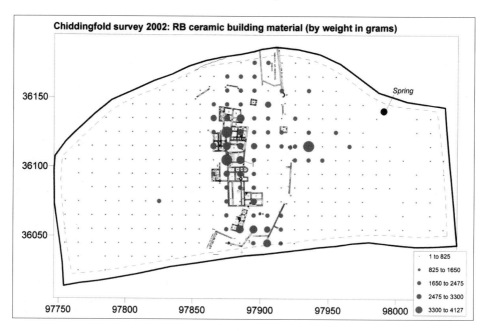

33 Chiddingfold: distribution of ceramic building material over nineteenth century building plan. Drawing by David and Audrey Graham over plan after Cooper et al 1984

As a general rule, Surrey's river valleys do not seem to have been attractive to villa settlement. Beddington and Carshalton are near the Wandle or related streams; Abinger is on the Tillingbourne *(34)* and might perhaps have held the whole valley as an estate. On the Mole there is only Chatley Farm and perhaps Pachesham (near Leatherhead) and Pixham (near Dorking). The last two can be postulated only from finds of building material which may have been reused on a non-villa site. There are occasional suggestions of a villa at Stoke D'Abernon church but the supposed crop marks on the manor house lawn are unconvincing and not supported by any other evidence. The Wey and Blackwater valleys (the latter forms the western county boundary) also seem to lack villas except for the Farnham buildings and possibly a site at Tongham.

The most important area for villas may have been the Fertile Greensand Belt or a somewhat broader area around it running along south of the Downs. There are known or likely villas at Titsey, Bletchingley, Abinger, Compton, Binscombe near Godalming, and Puttenham. Perhaps Farnham might also be counted in this group. A few others might be suggested; for instance the local place-name Flore near Godstone should be derived from a Saxon word for a mosaic or tessellated pavement, and it may be anticipated that there is a villa associated with the Doods Farm tileworks near Reigate. Others might be expected in the Churt Corridor west of Godalming and a mention of tesserae suggests another possibility near the known cremation cemetery at Haslemere.

There may have been villas at about four or five kilometre intervals along south of the Downs.

There were also villas on the Weald Clay, including Surrey's best known villa at Rapsley near Ewhurst. Recent work by the Surrey County Archaeological Unit has suggested that there was another nearby in the Cranleigh area. The evidence suggests that some of the clay areas may have been opened up to settlement as a result of road construction, for example Rapsley and Cranleigh villas in the Rowhook branch corridor and perhaps the area north and west of Guildford around the Broad Street/Barnwood villa. The group of buildings at Chiddingfold is also in the Weald Clay region, although the actual site is on a sandy hilltop *(33)*. If this was a villa it would be easily the largest in Surrey, and an alternative explanation can be offered, that it was an isolated religious complex. The idea is considered in greater detail later on in this book.

Taken altogether, the evidence suggests a total of 30-40 villas, although no more than about 20 can be regarded as reasonably certain, including bath-houses and sites such as Chiddingfold and Chatley Farm where alternative explanations are possible. 35 villas would match the total of the main landowners recorded in Domesday Book for Surrey, although the comparison is probably not very meaningful. If a villa is seen as the equivalent of a medieval manor then there should be many more than 35. In other areas it has been calculated that a villa estate might be no more than 50-100ha, although this would be on relatively good soils. If this was applied to Surrey, even if restricted to the Fertile Greensand Belt and other good soils, it would suggest that there are still a good number of villas to find. Clearly there is a need for much more fieldwork.

When the siting of the known villas is examined in detail, it can be seen that they show a definite tendency to be set at or near geological boundaries. This may be an indication of a desire to exploit a number of different subsoils, capable of providing a range of products or habitats. Soils in these locations will also have been naturally mixed, by run-off from the hills, probably leading to greater fertility. Such geological junctions also often give rise to springs. There seem to be two main groups of villas in Surrey; those on or adjacent to alluvium, river gravels or the Thanet Sand; and those on or more usually adjacent to heavy subsoils, especially the London Clay, Clay with Flints or Weald Clay. Presumably there was a marked difference in the economy of these groups, but our evidence is too poor to be able to say what it was with any degree of certainty. It would be reasonable to assume that a use of woodland, possibly including for grazing animals such as pigs, figured more strongly in the second group. Areas apparently without villas are of considerable interest: there is a marked avoidance of river valleys in general, and particularly the wide river terrace gravels along the Wey and the Thames. This suggests that there is little reason to suppose use of river transport, as is sometimes claimed. The central chalk area (from the Mole to the Wey), the Bagshot Beds, and the Lower

Greensand (except around Puttenham) also seem to have been avoided for the most part.

The distribution of villas strongly implies that they were to be found in particular circumstances, and that therefore the traveller in Roman Surrey would have been conscious of different zones or landscapes, among them typical villa country. There is, however, not much other evidence for the Roman-period landscape: a little is known about what grew around the towns, as noted above, but otherwise we are restricted to information about the plans of a few fields or enclosures, some not necessarily Roman. There are only a few informative aerial photographs because the soils and ground cover are generally unhelpful. The best areas would be the gravels, but Heathrow Airport is at the centre of the main gravel region which causes difficulties for aerial archaeologists! Nonetheless the best evidence comes mostly from sand and gravel areas as a result of large-scale excavations in advance of mineral extraction. This includes the sites at Thorpe Lea Nurseries *(30)*, Wey Manor Farm, and around Runfold near Farnham. On the other hand, testing of some gravel areas has failed to locate evidence for Roman period activity, such as an area around the Beddington villa and sites south of the London–Silchester road in the Shepperton area. This last place includes a word meaning sheep in its name, which is perhaps a hint that we may conclude that some of the gravel areas were used for pasture. Aerial photographic evidence indicates the presence of field systems on the chalk hills either side of the Mole Gap, of the small square kind usually called 'Celtic'. Some of them can still be traced on the ground, with difficulty. They may have been in use in the Roman period but this cannot yet be demonstrated. Dating is also a problem with field systems occasionally noted on heathland, including one system marked out by slight earthworks near the Walton Heath villa. In general, though, there is so little evidence from the heathlands that the most likely use was as poor grazing land.

This makes it very difficult to imagine the appearance of the Roman period countryside. The area shown on *colour plate 1* illustrates the problem very well: it is as though we have one or two very small pieces of this jigsaw but no way of telling what the rest of the area was like. Similarly, is it acceptable to take the evidence from the gravels or the chalk and apply it to different subsoils? Should we postulate settlements as centres of tamed countryside or settlements as islands in areas with much less management? Were some parts of the county still quite 'wild'? Northern art galleries are full of eighteenth- and nineteenth-century paintings of romantic 'wild' Surrey; we have already heard of the 'black desert' of the Bagshot heathlands and as modern experience shows, the natural state of much of the county is to be covered in trees.

At present therefore we can only work from the known distribution of settlement sites and what we know of the soils with analogies drawn from what is known of their later use, hardly a satisfactory state of affairs. It is probably reasonable to postulate open gravel terrace landscapes, part farmed and part pasture, large areas of heathland and of woodland, some open downland. A Roman writer, had he been interested, could no doubt have recorded zones in the same way as Stamp and Willats centuries later. He would also have recognised changes through time. The Roman period covers nearly 400 years and we can dimly see some of these changes, for example the coming of villas, which seems usually not to have happened until the second century. There is also some evidence to suggest that there was a considerable change in the landscape, around about the end of the second century, although maybe the result of a process covering quite a number of years. This saw the pattern of irregular fields which had continued from the Iron Age change to one of rectangular fields, about twice as long as broad. It can be seen at Thorpe Lea Nurseries *(30)* and is known at places throughout the London region and indeed in other parts of the western Empire. Clearly there must have been changes in the way the land was worked, and perhaps in ownership too. The reasons are not yet understood. The evidence is mostly from the gravels, and so it is not clear if other zones were affected in the same way.

The fact that villas are only found in some of the landscape zones raises interesting questions about villa estates. Were they also confined to certain zones? Other Roman-period settlement evidence appears to favour the Thames-side gravels and the spring line north and south of the Downs, in both cases associated with somewhat more fertile soils, so how do these sites relate to villas and the other zones? All our evidence suggests that from the beginning of modern human occupation of the county, in the Mesolithic (from about 8000 BC), people have utilised the different resources made available by so many different subsoils and topographical situations. Over the centuries this has given rise to a marked north–south tendency in land-use patterns, shown for example by many ancient routes and by many Surrey parishes, on both sides of the Downs. These parishes are likely to have grown out of earlier land-holdings and it can be no accident that they often form long strips, very narrow from east to west, allowing them to cut across different subsoils and thereby have access to the different resources available.

It is by no means unlikely that some of the parish boundaries fossilise much earlier land divisions, some of them in existence in the Roman period or even earlier. If this is the case, then the north–south tendency may have been just as strong in the Roman period, although it would be difficult to demonstrate. Effectively therefore this would cut across some or all of the zones noted. Consideration of villa estates commonly starts from the basis of circles at a standard distance from the villa. It would be reasonable to take a villa like Abinger and assume an estate within the Tillingbourne valley *(34)*; indeed in view of the apparent importance of the villa perhaps much of the valley might be included. But Surrey's strong historical north–south emphasis suggests that a different pattern should also be considered, of an estate running from the top of the Downs and south well into the Weald.

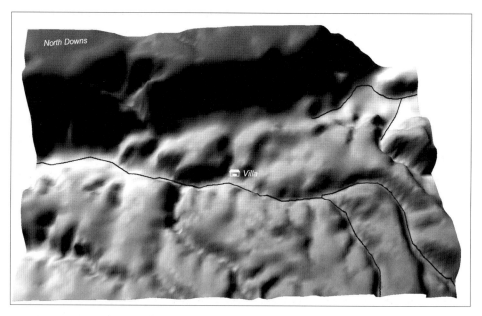

34 The setting of the Abinger villa in the Tillingbourne valley. The North Downs scarp is at the top of the page. Vertical heights are exaggerated. *Digital terrain map: David and Audrey Graham*

A further point may be considered: pre- and post-Roman use of the Weald for transhumance is taken for granted. Why should it be switched off in the Roman period and then on again? This suggests a very different purpose for places like Rapsley and its new partner near Cranleigh, almost like successors to the hillforts controlling and supporting the transhumance routes. They could then be seen as effectively forerunners of the more permanent settlement in the Weald in the later Saxon period. Places like Chiddingfold and Dunsfold, where there is evidence for Roman period occupation are also relevant. Rob Poulton has pointed out that enclosures and clearings are indicated by the Saxon names of these places (*falod* and *leah*), perhaps an indication that they were already in existence in the Roman period. It would also be relevant to note that Crutchfield (somewhere in the Reigate area) and Limpsfield both have *feld* elements, meaning some sort of clearing, combined with British words, suggesting continuity.

A lack of understanding of likely villa estates means that discussion of the functions of the villas is difficult. It is clear, however, that they were not simply country houses. They are usually assumed to have had associated estates and be productive in some way, but not necessarily having agriculture as their prime purpose. Thus the Ashtead Common villa seems to have been primarily concerned with tile production; Farnham may well be associated with the local pottery industry; Rapsley probably had a nearby stone quarry and tileworks.

The function of others must be guessed from their locations, but they do not often show signs of great wealth. Some of the clay group may have been centres of forestry estates, or at least had woodland products as a part of their economy.

It has been demonstrated that in the medieval period the proximity of the London market caused estates to develop specialisms. Key factors are held to be reasonably effective 'policing', unified coinage, a system of contracts, a good road system, and standard weights and measures, all of which apply to the Roman period. Places like the Ashtead tileworks are evidence for specialisation, but it is of course more difficult to find surviving evidence where the produce was organic. London would have been a big market in the Roman period, at upwards of 20,000 people, and would have required large amounts of grain, animals, fuel and timber. It has been calculated that the city needed 100,000 tons of wood for fuel annually around 1300; the population may have been as high as 100,000 as well, indicating an average requirement of around 1,000 tons per person. A similar calculation for the Roman period would then suggest a need for up to 30,000 tons. As well as fuel there would have been huge requirements for timber and underwood. Probably the bulk of London's grain would have come from some area other than Surrey, particularly north Kent and the Verulamium area. Surrey may have been better suited to animals, and it would have been very suited to woodland industries.

Trees grow quickly in Surrey, especially on the abundant clay; the county is the most wooded in England, with nearly 25% cover. As we have seen, growing trees is the only sensible use for some of the clays. This was true even close to London, in the area north of Croydon; in the last century the naturalist J.E. Lousley drew attention to the surviving remnants of the oaks of the great North Wood (surviving in the place-name Norwood). Penge, nearby, is recorded as a big wood in the medieval period but its name is a rare British survival meaning something like 'chief wood' which implies an impressive feature in the early Saxon period and therefore surely present in Roman times. It has been suggested above that we may even have a named wood, Verlucionium, in this part of the county, if it fell within the *civitas* of the Cantiaci.

Writing in 1826 Johann Heinrich von Thünen considered the requirements of an idealised state. Taking account of transport needs (not then so different from the Roman period) he suggested that the most cost-effective use of the second zone out from a city would be for woodland. He recognised that the ideal pattern would be altered by such things as climate and soils, but it can be seen that Surrey would fit this pattern well. Some authors still write as though land remains clear once trees are cut down, but of course this is not the case unless a specific new land use is intended. Trees and underwood can be a crop like any other, although on a longer cycle. There is clear evidence for tree management in Britain from long before the Roman period and Roman writers describe coppicing practice. This all suggests that it is right to conclude that the London Clay and perhaps the Clay with Flints probably across much of Roman Surrey were used for woodland and this was regarded as a major resource. The Weald Clay was perhaps too far out from London and the towns to be used for production at this stage, except perhaps for very large timbers when required. Little can yet be said about the trees themselves, although oak was no doubt most common on the clays and analysis of charcoal from the Ashtead Common tileworks suggested oak. Similar analysis at the Overwey pottery kilns near Tilford gave a more varied picture: ash, birch, hazel or oak, which perhaps reflects tree cover on the local greensand. Tony Clark noted the absence of pine and argued that it would surely have been used if locally available. It may have been missing after the Mesolithic or a bit later and not reintroduced until more modern times.

How was the woodland industry organised? In view of its importance it is reasonable to draw parallels with the pottery and tile industries which we can see were organised on a large scale. Some of the workforce may have been peripatetic, for example charcoal burners, but since this was a big industry, surely working round on a coppice rotation system, permanent bases are likely. We readily accept the idea of agricultural workers walking out and back to their fields on a regular basis. It must be possible that some of the roadside settlements in clay areas served as centres for the woodland industry, and also some of the villas.

As we have seen, grain in various forms was supplied to the local towns and perhaps also to London. It presumably came mostly from the more fertile land perhaps especially the gravels, which may even have been controlled for this purpose. Beddington for example produced spelt wheat, bread wheat and barley, but of course we have no way of being certain where it was then used. We also need much more evidence to be able to understand the scale of production and if different areas specialised in different crops. Some of the production was used to make beer, probably in the so-called 'corn driers' which have been reintrepreted as malting kilns, such as those known or possible at Farleigh Court near Chelsham, Hurst Park near Weybridge and in Ewell.

There may have been some unusual specialist production areas. Margaret Gelling has drawn attention to the origins of the place-name Croydon, which probably means 'saffron valley' incorporating the words *croh* and *denu*. The first element is especially interesting as it comes from the Latin *crocus*. This should refer to *crocus sativus*, the autumn crocus, which had various uses in the Roman world. It provided a dye (yellow or deep red (derived from the stigma)), an aromatic oil and was apparently even mixed with sweet wine and sprayed at theatres, giving a costly fragrance. Gelling wonders how the Latin word came to be used by Anglo-Saxon people and notes that it is in the centre of an area with other British loan words and indications of Britons present with Saxons.

Had it been a local industry, still marking the landscape, rather like Mitcham's famous lavender fields centuries later? As a yellow dye can be obtained more cheaply from a native plant called weld the idea is perhaps unlikely but it is an intriguing possibility. The recently discovered tin of expensive ointment or cream on the Tabard Square site in Southwark shows that it would not be entirely out of context.

The town evidence already cited indicates that the expected animals would have been seen in Roman Surrey: cattle, sheep, pigs, horses, dogs, and so on. But once again we cannot at present say if particular areas specialised, or if the stock improved through the course of the Roman period as seems to be the case elsewhere. In general there is little evidence for hunting, and very little sign that game was supplied to the towns. A few of the villas have relevant evidence: deer at Farnham, Titsey and Compton for instance (red and roe deer are represented), and hare at Titsey. Interestingly, there seems to be no record of wild boar. Only recently have archaeological techniques improved sufficiently to make the recovery of fish bones reasonably common so it is not possible to say what part fish played in the diet. A possible late Roman fish weir was recorded during gravel extraction at Ferry Lane Shepperton (although it might be Saxon or Saxo-Norman); there were posts forming a V-shape set across the channel probably with a basket trap in the jaws. Other things are largely invisible; for instance honey must have been important as the only sweetener, and beeswax was used in various ways. A special pot (basically a very large jar with many perforations), made in the Alice Holt/Farnham potteries is thought to have been intended for use as a bee hive, but it is not a common find. One is known from Ewell. More recent analogy shows that hives could have been made from reused amphorae or, of course, perishable materials.

As sheep were ubiquitous in Roman Britain and as we have evidence from several sites it is probably reasonable to assume that they were widespread in Surrey. They are recorded in towns at Southwark, Staines and Ewell, in the countryside at Beddington, Titsey, Farnham and Binscombe. They marked tiles used at Wanborough and Rapsley, the latter probably from the Wykehurst kilns and perhaps not surprisingly showing signs of foot rot *(35)*. The terra-cotta pine cones at Rapsley *(colour plate 10)* should be associated with Attis, appropriate for a stock-raising place (and especially for sheep). Although there is little sign of them among the animal bones these hardly survived the ground conditions and sheep were overwintered locally in recent times. Sheep grazing would have been a good use for Surrey's extensive heathland (although in places it could have taken cattle too). There seem to have been special heath sheep later on: around 1800 Stevenson recorded that a 'singular breed of small ill-formed sheep then entirely occupied the extensive heaths in the west of the county'. A later description makes them sound almost prehistoric: 'black or brown faced, thin and high on the leg'. Some of the Roman-period evidence taken to indicate sheep may actually be goat; it is very difficult to tell them

35 Tile fragment from Rapsley, with animal print thought to have been made by a sheep with foot rot. *Photograph: Rosamond Hanworth*

apart by examining bones. For this reason archaeological reports often refer to 'ovicaprids'. We cannot therefore say if there were herds of goats or if goats were kept in settlements for their milk, as is perhaps likely.

Sheep probably became increasingly important for wool through the course of the Roman period, and as noted above, Ewell may have been a centre for the woollen industry. British products achieve a high grade in the Diocletianic Price Edict of AD 301, which attempted to control prices in the Empire. The *birrus* (a sort of duffle coat) scored highly and both first and second grade wool rugs (*tapetia*) were the best in the Roman world. This suggests a means of controlling the quality of production. If the idea of Surrey produce reaching the wider Empire seems unlikely, then consider the case of the medieval merchant, Francesco di Marco Datini, of Prato in Italy, who in the years around AD 1400 imported English cloth, among which was specified *panni di Guildiforte* (Guildford cloth).

SEVEN

VILLAS

Although they must have been the exception rather than the rule in the country-side, the villas deserve detailed attention as an important part of our evidence. The term will be understood here to mean a rural building with at least stone foundations, tiled roofs, and rectangularity, together with extras such as under-floor heating, painted wall plaster, and baths. As we have seen, we know or can postulate 30-40 villas, but in fact only about 20 can be regarded as reasonably certain (for the location of the sites discussed below, see *1*).

Consideration of some aspects is made more difficult because very few Surrey villas have been excavated to modern standards, and only at Rapsley *(36)* has most of the site been excavated and published, with an imaginative attempt to understand the surroundings. Even here we lack the cemetery and certainly do not have all the information about the buildings; there may even be others to find. Publication of the very extensive work at Beddington *(45)* has been eagerly awaited for several years, particularly for what it can tell us of the surroundings of the main buildings, so rarely studied. Recent work at Barnwood School near the Broad Street Common villa is also of importance in this context *(42)*.

Except for Rapsley (and perhaps Broad Street/Barnwood and Beddington), we mostly lack the evidence to discuss development of the villas through time. Old reports make clear the inadequacy of excavation methods, and the reports themselves rarely provide enough information to make possible reinterpreta-tion in the light of current knowledge. For example, a pot at Ashtead was said to be placed under the floor as a foundation deposit and as such would of course be valuable dating evidence. The way the site was dug, however, and the difficult ground conditions (52) suggest that it is equally possible that the pot was a later insertion into the floor, perhaps for use as a money box or as part of a ritual. Several of Lowther's reports show internal inconsistencies which cannot now be untangled because there are no original records surviving, but which should make us very wary of attempting to reinterpret what he tells us, and the same is true for many of the early excavations.

Close dating for most of the villas is therefore not possible, and in what follows dates are usually only given when they are soundly based. Material from each site can be used as an indication of the length of occupation, but it should be kept in mind that this does not necessarily relate to the villa as such. One value of the Rapsley excavation is that it shows how a site may have material dating to well before there are any signs of villa buildings. For what it is worth, it is possible that the villas at Abinger, Ashtead and Walton Heath were begun before AD 100, but most are likely to be later, starting some time in the second century. In general, they mostly seem to end by the middle of the fourth century. Some apparently start particularly late: Farnham and Chatley Farm were evidently built in the fourth century, but at both of these sites we may only have later additions to larger complexes. Some places have Iron Age material in sufficient quantity to suggest pre-Roman occupation; this tends to be the sites on the good soils. What this might mean in terms of continuity is discussed later.

The Rapsley villa was discovered by chance in 1956, and after some work by others the site was excavated over several seasons by Rosamond Hanworth and published in 1968. Among other things, it is important for placing a villa in the context of its associated buildings; for the information about its development; for the way it shows a stone-built bath-house with attached timber-built rooms (which would probably have been missed by early excavators); and for the way in which the plans are carefully recorded and not 'tidied up' to give a misleading impression of regularity.

Five main periods of occupation were recognised (36). No buildings were located for Period I but debris in pits showed that there was occupation around AD 80. In Period II (about AD 120-200) there was a small rectangular timber building (3 on 36) with three rooms and a corridor. It was burnt down about AD 200, possibly as part of a clearance of the site for the next phase. Fragmentary remains of a masonry structure were also found to the south-east. Period III (AD 200–220) saw the first villa-like buildings: an aisled structure (1: only the southern end was available for excavation) and a separate bath-house (6), divided by a fence or wall; and on the baths side of the division a small apsidal shrine (5). There were also boundary walls with a drainage ditch along the southern side. The shrine had a stone base (37) perhaps for a basin (it had a drain and traces of a coating), and around it signs of a timber outer protective structure with a tessellated floor. The bath-house had two timber

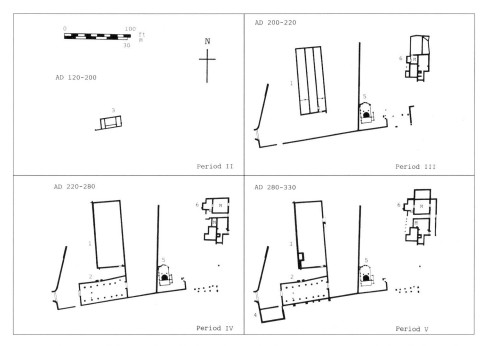

36 Development of the Rapsley villa through time. 'M' – mosaic. *Drawing: Audrey Graham, after Smith 1980*

37 The shrine (Building 5) at Rapsley. *Photograph: Rosamond Hanworth*

38 Rapsley: baths furnace drain. *Photograph: Rosamond Hanworth*

rooms at its northern end and a simple mosaic floor. Two imbrex tile drains *(38)* fed into a rubble drain which was seven feet wide by Period IV. The aisled building (1) showed signs of partitioning in the aisles and traces of tiled or tessellated floors.

Building 1 needed repairs but still partly collapsed and so was rebuilt with good masonry but apparently without aisles about 4m to the north of its original site in Period IV (which ran from about AD 220 to 280). A new aisled building (2) was constructed at right angles to the new Building 1; it may have been a workshop, as a hearth and associated signs of metalworking as well as a dump of tesserae were found there. The bath block (6) was turned into a small house, with new stone-founded rooms replacing the timber ones at the northern end and a proper mosaic *(colour plate 2)* set into a wide tessellated surround in the principal room. This room had no underfloor heating; a severely burnt patch on the floor, repaired in Period V, suggests the use of a brazier. Rooms near the former bath furnace were still heated but there no longer seem to have been baths as such. Gradually the new floors in the northern rooms sank into the badly backfilled sleeper-beam trenches used for the timber building *(colour plate 4)*.

The final period (V) lasted from about AD 280 to 330. A new small building (4) was constructed outside the complex but using its wall at the south-west corner of the site; its three new walls all had very deep foundations. Buttresses now supported Building 2. Three more rooms were added to the house (6),

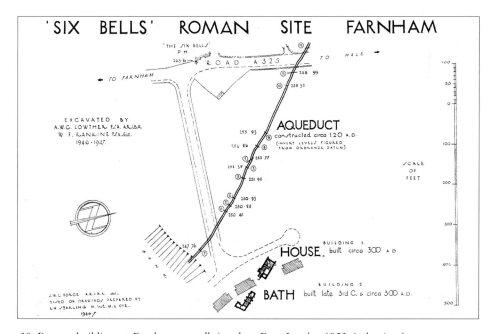

39 Roman buildings at Farnham: overall site plan. *From Lowther 1953-4, drawing 1*

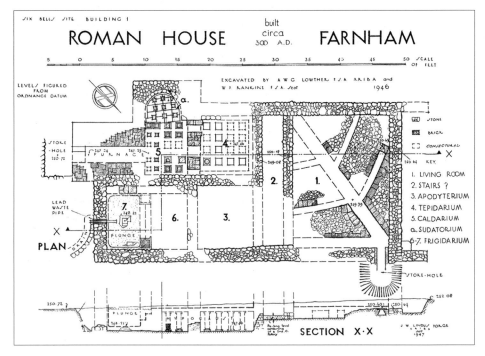

40 Farnham 'house' plan. *From Lowther 1953-4, drawing 2*

one with a cobbled floor, and it took on the appearance of a winged corridor villa. At the end of the occupation the house and Building 1 were apparently destroyed by fire, which may have been part of a deliberate act of abandonment. It was noted that the floors of the house had been kept very clean, and tiles from the floor of one room had been removed before the fire.

Rapsley now looks less isolated in the Weald with the discovery of another possible villa near Cranleigh, not far to the west. Although the site has only been tested as part of a site evaluation exercise, it had stone foundations and associated Roman pottery including samian, so identification as a villa is reasonably certain. The new discovery is a reminder that the apparent isolation of the building complex at Chiddingfold, further west, may be more apparent than real. The Chiddingfold site *(33)* was excavated in 1883 and in 1888-9 and has been interpreted as a villa. There was apparently a large complex of Roman period buildings, whose layout gives the impression of being an accumulation of additional buildings with no overall planning. Associated material suggests activity mostly in the mid-second to the later third centuries and so there are likely to be several phases but these cannot now be untangled. There are known to have been hypocausts in some rooms and one apsidal-ended room is likely to have been a bath. Some rooms are known to have had red tessellated floors but there is no sign that there were mosaics. This impression was

1 *Previous page* Stane Street heading south from Ockley; the line can be seen continuing where the modern road swings away at the top of the photograph. *Courtesy Surrey County Council*

2 *Left* Mosaic floor in the Rapsley villa. *Drawing by David Neal*

3 *Below* Phallic pendants from the Puttenham (built-in loop) and Reigate areas; the Chiddingfold ibis; 'ear of corn' from Wanborough. *Photograph: Brian Wood, courtesy Surrey Archaeological Society and Guildford Museum*

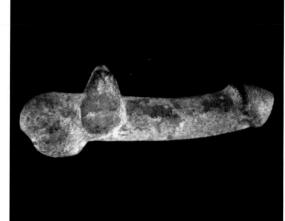

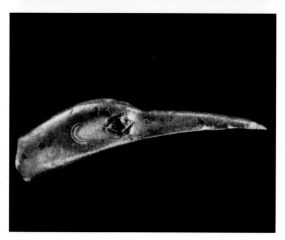

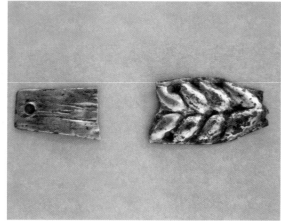

4 *Above* Rapsley
Building 6: tessellated
floor sinking into earlier
features. *Photograph:
Rosamond Hanworth*

5 *Right* Mosaic floor in
the Abinger villa.
*Drawing by Steve Cosh and
David Neal*

6 *Left* Mosaic floor in the Walton Heath villa. *Courtesy Surrey Archaeological Society*

7 *Below, clockwise from top left* Brooches: disc, Rapsley; bird, Puttenham area; disc, Wanborough; wheel, Binscombe. *Photograph: Brian Wood, courtesy Surrey Archaeological Society and Guildford Museum*

Opposite, clockwise from top left:
8 Ashtead: 'dog and stag' tile. *Photograph: author*

9 Ashtead: flue-tile with mismatched pattern. *Photograph: John Hampton*

10 Backworth brooch, Wanborough; fragments of mural crowns, Rapsley and Chiddingfold; terracotta pine cones, Rapsley. *Photograph: Brian Wood, courtesy Surrey Archaeological Society and Guildford Museum*

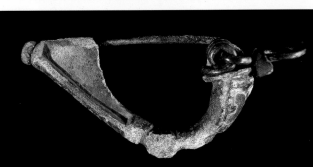

11 Above Details of the Wanborough head-dresses. *Photograph: Brian Wood, courtesy Surrey Archaeological Society and Guildford Museum*

12 Below Some of the Wanborough sceptres and a head-dress from Farley Heath. *Photograph: Brian Wood, courtesy Surrey Archaeological Society and Guildford Museum*

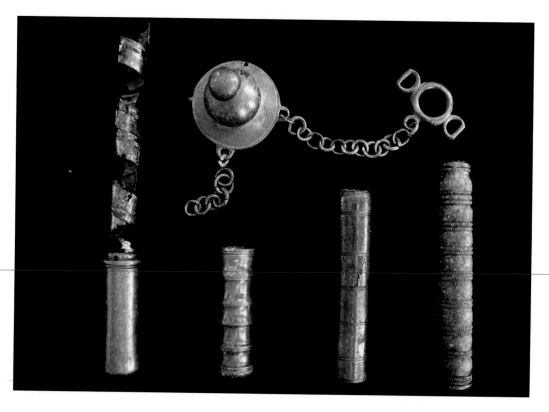

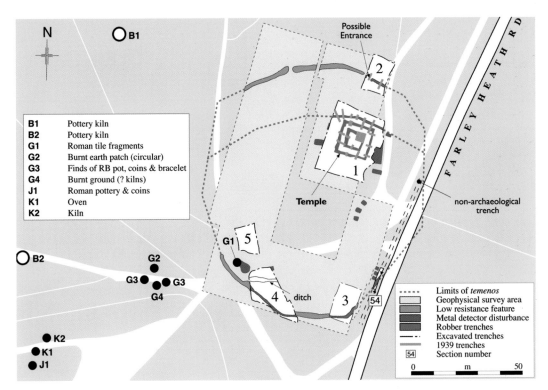

13 Above Plan of features at the Farley Heath temple site. *Courtesy Surrey County Archaeological Unit*

14 Right Farley Heath: miniature altars (1, 2); *cyathus* (3) (10cm scale refers); brooches (4–9, 11–14); ring (10). Nineteenth-century drawings by Benjamin Nightingale, *courtesy Administrators of the Haverfield Bequest*; side views of 1 & 2, and 3, *drawing: Giles Pattison*

Overleaf
15 (left) & *16 (right)* Nineteenth century illustrations of finds from the Titsey villa. *From Leveson-Gower 1869, plates II and III*

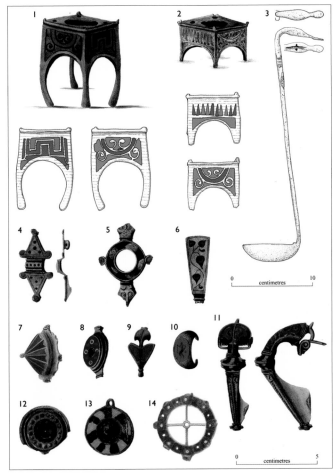

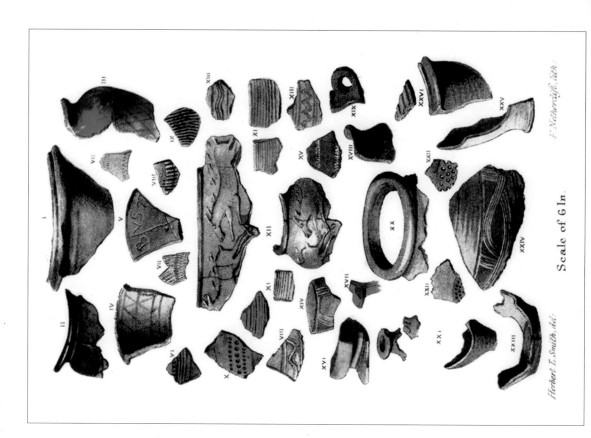

Herbert L. Smith. del.

Scale of 6 In.

F. Netheraift. lith.

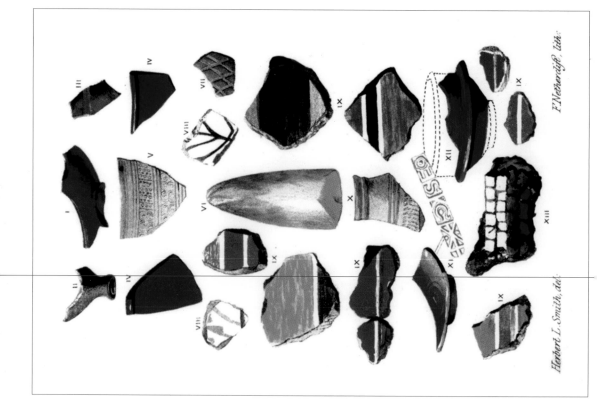

Herbert L. Smith. del.

F. Netheraift. lith.

strengthened by the results of recent detailed fieldwalking, which confirmed the basic size and area of the buildings and located building materials including red tile tesserae but no other colours. A possible explanation for the site as a religious complex is explored later on.

Evidence for the Farnham villa was first noted in 1925, in the form of a pit with building material. The site was excavated by Lowther and others in 1946-7 in advance of development, with a workforce partly composed of German prisoners of war. The 'pit' was shown to be a section across a linear feature and interpreted as an aqueduct *(39)* supplying a pottery workshop. It was dated to the mid second century and backfilled with large amounts of third and fourth-century pottery, so was evidently not in use when the buildings were constructed. Two buildings were found, described as a house *(40)* and a bath *(41)*. The bath-house was said to have two phases, the first late third century (dated by the layer of pottery waste material through which its foundations were dug), followed by refurbishment in the early fourth century when the apsidal plunge bath was added and plaster (from the earlier phase?) was used as make up for it. This later phase was seen as contemporary with construction of the 'house'.

Part of the bath-house was constructed over a raft of rammed chalk set on timber piles apparently in order to cope with the unstable land, and a number of wall stubs on both buildings were interpreted as buttresses required for the

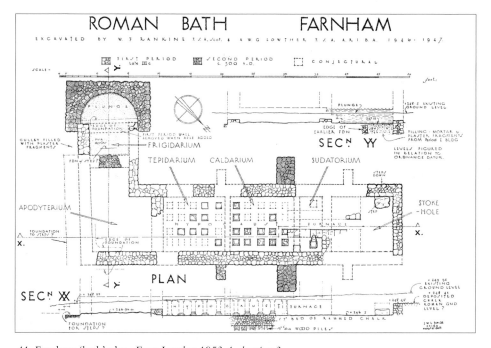

41 Farnham 'bath' plan. *From Lowther 1953-4, drawing 3*

same reason. But the plans strongly suggest that these stubs were actually parts of more rooms, which might be expected as there would otherwise be too much bath provision in the two buildings. The 'house' has one big heated room at the north end and the plan looks very much as though the main building might be expected to continue to the north. The bath-house has a close parallel at Compton *(49)*, but there it is just across one end of a villa. The site report notes that digging conditions in the winter of 1946-7 were unpleasant and site photographs suggest that excavation continued little if at all beyond the area planned, so wall continuations could easily have been missed.

In 1971 last-minute salvage excavation in advance of housing development recorded just enough evidence to suggest the presence of a villa at Binscombe near Godalming. Little could be recovered of the plan but there were some traces of timber-framed structures which probably preceded a stone-founded building with a substantial drain. The latter would have been very necessary on the site; the archaeological excavation was finally abandoned when it became totally waterlogged. Only two possible rooms were noted, one of which had the skeleton of a small elderly horse lying amongst the rubble from its collapse. The horse, which was about 25 years old, had apparently been hacked across its shins so that it could no longer stand, which perhaps suggests a rather dramatic end to the occupation. Unfortunately the event is not well-dated, so explanations can only be speculative. The finds mark this site out as high status: among the pottery were mortaria and continental imports including over 50 samian vessels; there were ironstone and some red tile tesserae; and a fine brooch *(colour plate 7)*. Together they indicate activity on site from the second to the fourth centuries.

The Compton villa is better known, at least in terms of its plan *(49)*. It was found early in 1914 in a kitchen garden extension: 'the men ran into a mass of loose flints and building material and a little further on into solid masonry'. Work was stopped and the site was excavated in 1915. Although this is not made clear in the report, it must be likely that the kitchen garden work actually removed part of the south-east corner of the building, where a second projecting wing might have been expected. Photographs suggest that the baths end was the first part to be excavated. There are a few signs of changes through time: a wall inserted into the baths (between rooms J and K), and perhaps the odd thickening of the wall between F and B. A few pieces of flooring survived, including a patch of red tesserae in the northern corridor and tile paving in the southern *(50)*.

The villa on Broad Street Common was first excavated in 1829, when a row of five rooms fronted by a corridor was found *(42;* 'Sibthorpe's villa'). There was a mosaic in the central room, a hint that the villa was actually much larger. Unfortunately it was apparently removed to Clandon House (the land was owned by the Earl of Onslow) and has not been seen since; no record of its appearance is known. Nearly 170 years later, excavation in advance of development in the

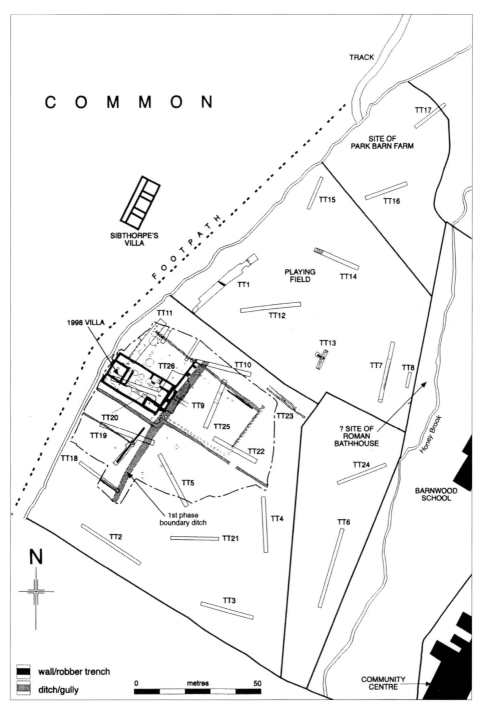

COMMON

TT17

SITE OF
PARK BARN FARM

SIBTHORPE'S
VILLA

TT15

TT16

F O O T P A T H

PLAYING
FIELD

TT1

TT14

TT12

1998 VILLA

TT11

TT13

TT10

TT7   TT8

TT26

TT9

TT23

? SITE OF
ROMAN
BATHHOUSE

Honey Brook

TT20

TT25

TT19

TT22

TT18

TT24

BARNWOOD
SCHOOL

TT5

1st phase
boundary ditch

TT4

TT6

N

TT2

TT21

TT3

wall/robber trench

ditch/gully

0   metres   50

COMMUNITY
CENTRE

42 Roman buildings at Broad Street Common and Barnwood School. *Courtesy Surrey County Archaeological Unit* grounds of the nearby Barnwood School has added new information, including what must be an associated building. The new work by the Surrey County Archaeological Unit was on quite a large scale, and it was noted that there was virtually no indication of prehistoric activity. The earliest features were some late first or early second-century cremation burials, presumably indicating nearby occupation. They probably preceded a wide boundary ditch dug in the first part of the second century which is likely to have been contemporary with a timber building. The latter was marked by parallel lines of posts at right angles to the stone-founded building that succeeded it. The big ditch was also filled in before the new building was constructed.

In plan this looks like an aisled building, although the aisles are apparently not continuous but made up of several rooms. There were no surviving floors. An extra wall at the south-west end was possibly a foundation for steps up at the front. The building had deep foundations of flint-packed trenches, especially so (about 1.5m) for the front corner rooms; it is suggested that these were towers. Walls in both directions continued the line of the front end of the building, presumably enclosing the space in which it stood. There were also ditches marking out an enclosure around and in front of the building, and later a roughly square area here marked out by substantial post-holes on two sides. These seem to be too big for a fence but it is difficult to think of any other purpose. The area marked out was generally clean so there is nothing to help assess its use. A loading area for whatever was kept in the 'towers' might be suggested but if that were the case it might be expected that the area would have been cobbled on this clay subsoil. In the later third or the fourth century large deep pits were dug along the line of the aisles, in some cases cutting right through the flint foundations. Presumably the building was demolished at this time, unless these were very drastic repairs and alterations. A general spread of fourth-century material suggests continued activity somewhere in the vicinity. The site is divided from the 1829 villa by a stream, but this may be part of the artificial boundary of the medieval royal park. It must be likely that the two sites were really one complex, which may have included a separate bath-house suggested by the finds from limited excavation nearby.

North from Broad Street Common, an Iron Age and Roman site at Lightwater was studied in seven seasons of excavation in the 1980s. Unfortunately there has been little publication as yet. There seem to have been Iron Age ditches and slag from metalworking that continued into the early Roman period. There were also later Roman ditches and a number of third- and fourth-century buildings. Some reports talk of earlier buildings and speak of large quantities of samian and Oxfordshire ware which suggests a high-status site. It is to be hoped that publication will make possible a balanced assessment of this site, of importance because of its location within the Bagshot Beds area.

The site at Abinger on the Tillingbourne (*34*) was excavated (badly) in 1877 (*3*) and much more recently in 1995-7, when the well-preserved remains of four or five rooms with a possible corridor to the south were found. One of these rooms had a mosaic floor *(colour plate 5)*. Trenches a little to the west revealed the much more disturbed traces of further rooms, giving a possible length for the building of around 60m. There were also indications of walls down the slope to the south towards the Tillingbourne. This suggests a large villa with a main back range and long side wings, but the evidence is not clear enough for certainty. Publication should give a better understanding of the dating of the site and of its appointments, although the recent excavations were mostly confined to unstratified deposits.

The villa at Walton on the Hill was first located in a practice trench dug by the Public Schools Battalion in 1915, which cut through the bath *(48)*. At this time the site was in a field; by the time of excavation by Frere in 1938, continued by Lowther in 1939-40, the site was in a garden and could only be examined in gaps between the rose beds *(47)*. Writing up in wartime also caused difficulties. The result was a plan with a great deal of reconstruction and anomalies in the published report, such as different dates given for the phasing. There was probably a winged corridor villa with attached baths at the northern end, and a small detached circular building nearby. There are signs of two or three phases; a possibly hexagonal reception or dining room attached to the western side is likely to have been a late addition. This level of luxury has no Surrey parallel so it is encouraging that rather more of this room was examined than the others, making its identification reasonably certain. We may mourn the likely loss of a mosaic here. Contradictions in the report mean that dating is uncertain; there was probably some late Iron Age activity; an early wall about AD 100; then the villa in the later second or first half of the third century; destruction of the baths around AD 280-300; and perhaps some late rebuilding towards the end of the fourth century.

The nearby Walton Heath villa has had a long history of antiquarian endeavour, mostly destructive and to little positive effect. It was first noted in 1770, when it was being used as a quarry for building material. There were excavations in 1772, 1789, 1808 and 1856 when Pocock arranged for the mosaic to be recorded *(colour plate 6)*. This was fortunate, as it no longer exists. There were also some subsequent excavations. The 1856 plan *(2)* shows part of a substantial building with the location of the mosaic, and a 'deep pit' which was probably the bath-house. Several of the rooms are said to have had red tessellated floors and one report suggests that there was a hypocaust under the mosaic. There may have been a third villa in this Walton group, at Headley, a little to the west. Unpublished excavation there in 1959 seems to have traced walls and tile debris with associated fourth-century coins and pottery.

As we have seen, the Titsey villa was the first in Surrey to be recorded in any detail *(4)*. It was found in Titsey Park in 1847 and excavated in 1864 when Leveson Gower could trace the foundations as parch marks. He found what seems to be an aisled building developed into a winged corridor villa with a baths extension and a separate heated room at the opposite end. Its walls had the substantial foundations that seem to be characteristic of Surrey villas on clay subsoils. There were some traces of red tessellated flooring in situ and evidence for the former presence of a mosaic. The baths area is difficult to understand and likely to be a number of phases jumbled together. It was once interpreted as a *fullonica*, for the fulling of cloth, but this is unlikely. Recently geophysical survey has suggested that there was another winged corridor villa facing the original site about 60 metres away but divided from it by a stream and set higher, up a bank. There were also signs of a small building between the two buildings on the eastern side. It could perhaps have been a detached bath-house or a shrine.

West of Titsey, at Bletchingley, part of a bath-house was found in 1813 and recorded before being covered over. The early drawing shows two small rectangular rooms attached to two apsidal-ended rooms with hypocausts which were apparently full of Roman tiles when found. The site is said to have been subjected to treasure hunting in recent times; no finds have been reported. In 1996 geophysical survey located an extra wall but not enough to suggest that the bath-house was directly attached to a villa, although we can be certain that one will have existed nearby. North from Titsey, at Chelsham, a villa has been found recently by aerial photography, a rare occurrence in Surrey *(32)*. It seems to be a standard winged corridor villa with a detached building some way off; limited excavation in 1997 suggests that this was a bath-house with flint rubble walls and a lead pipe drain. Red tesserae were found centred on the villa site during fieldwalking. Finds from the site date from the second to the fourth centuries, with most of the pottery between third and fourth. There is no obvious water supply although Roman pottery was found near an existing pond well away from the buildings.

Lowther cut his archaeological teeth at the Ashtead Common villa, which was dug between 1926 and 1928 and published with commendable speed. As we have seen, the digging technique left a great deal to be desired *(5, 52)*, and the site conditions were often difficult on the clay. This is most unfortunate, as the site is very unusual; the villa plan has been described as unique among British villas, the detached bath-house is of a rare pattern and there are many other oddities. These deserve a full discussion which will be attempted at the end of this chapter. Although caution is necessary, it is likely that the plans we have *(43, 44)* are reasonably trustworthy and that building started in the later first century and the site was abandoned by the early third. It is, however, difficult to be sure of additions and changes through time. The villa had heated rooms and its own bath-house which seems to have been a later addition, and was apparently surrounded on at least three sides by a drain or gutter lined with tiles, probably essential on the sticky clay site. It is possible that the original bath-house was later adapted into a house, as happened at Rapsley, and it certainly underwent changes, including replastering. The buildings were

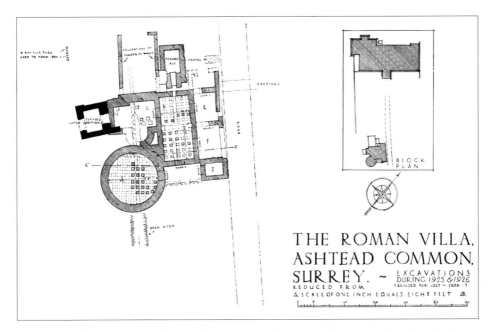

43 Ashtead Common: plan of Roman bath-house and its relationship to the villa. *From Lowther 1930*

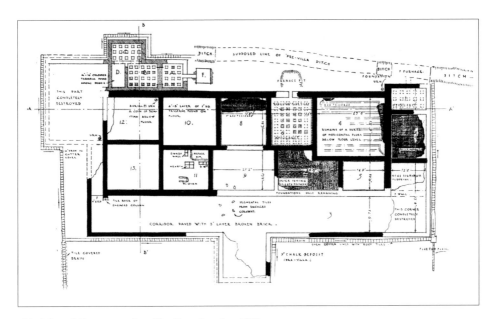

44 Ashtead Common: the villa. *From Lowther 1930*

obviously associated with the adjacent tile works and used many of its products. Excavations by John Hampton in 1964 at the tileworks found a right-angled piece of walling that may have been an enclosure round the villa or part of another building *(54, 55)*.

The close association of the villa and the tileworks is interesting as the buildings seem to be constructed to too high a standard to be simply intended for a manager while the owner lived on a more pleasant site. It would have been easy to find one not too far away, such as the Ashtead Church site where Lowther found evidence for another stone-founded building in 1933-4. This however seems to have dated to the third century and may even have been built with material taken from the Ashtead Common site. It was set in a ditched enclosure and had been cut by the later approach to the medieval manor. The walls had mostly been robbed, probably for material to use in the church, but finds included box flue-tile, roof tile and some wall plaster. This indicates a villa, and there is evidence nearby to suggest a larger complex.

The Chatley Farm site near Cobham was dug by Frere in 1942, when the site was found eroding into the Mole. Just three or four rooms of a bath-house had survived, dated AD 320-360. Two phases were suggested, with various changes interpreted as showing that the builders were struggling to make the heating system work. The bath-house is unusually late, and, as noted above, the site produced many different box flue-tile patterns that must have been reused from elsewhere. These are discussed in more detail in the next chapter. It is suggested that there was a villa to the east which has been lost to the action of the Mole. Pottery and tile has been found in the nearby field but small-scale excavation in 1979-80 failed to locate any evidence for structures, tending to confirm the idea of a lost villa. The pottery was dated late second to fourth century, and this together with its location suggests more widespread activity.

The site at Beddington was originally known only for its bath-house, found in 1871 during the extension of a sewage works. Work about 110 years later by the South-West London Unit of the Surrey Archaeological Society (now part of the Museum of London's Archaeological Service) found what remained of a villa and much of its surroundings *(45)*. The site had already been used through the Bronze and Iron Ages and there is a complicated sequence of features; it is unfortunate that we still await full publication so that they can be understood. The villa and bath-house are said to date from the mid second century, although the site was probably occupied from the later first until well into the fourth century. A cobbled area south of the bath-house was covered with a large amount of wall plaster considered to have fallen from an earlier clay and timber building for which there was otherwise no evidence. Three probable aisled buildings were found ('barns' 1-3), probably each a replacement for the previous one. The first and second were marked only by their aisle posts. A chalk and tufa block circular well with timber construction at its lowest levels was located immediately to the east of the latest barn.

bath-house

villa

N

'barn' 3

'barn' 2

'barn' 1

well

0   50
                                  m

45 Beddington: plan of features of all periods; the bath-house and villa plans are also shown separately for clarity. *Drawing: author, after Adkins* et al *1987*

There are some earlier records suggesting the presence of other stone buildings in the vicinity of the Beddington villa, and it is possible that the villa's burial ground was across the river, at the church site where a lead and a stone coffin have been found *(66)*. Not much further west, at Carshalton, excavation in advance of development has very recently located another possible villa *(46)*. There was evidence for one large stone-founded room and the presence of others beyond the excavated area. Associated finds included flue-tile and pottery suggesting late Iron Age to early Roman activity on site and a possible date for the villa from the second to the fourth centuries. Excavation was limited and the site has been preserved in situ.

We have enough evidence from all these villa sites to be able to make some generalisations. For example, an examination of the way they were placed in the landscape may help to understand if this mattered to our villa owners as it did elsewhere in the Empire. There is clear evidence for Roman villa owners appreciating views of landscape, such as the wall paintings in Italian villas. While it is difficult to prove that this approach also applied as far away as Britain, it is possible: high-ranking Roman officials did spend time in the province, some even as exiles, so the ideas current in their circles could have been transmitted to higher-ranking Britons. The same Romano-British 'upper class' would have been responsible for the building of temples, and there are signs that these were placed with an eye to their setting. This may have derived as much from earlier visions of the landscape and the place of people within it

46 Carshalton: probable villa from the south-west. *Courtesy of Sutton Archaeological Services*

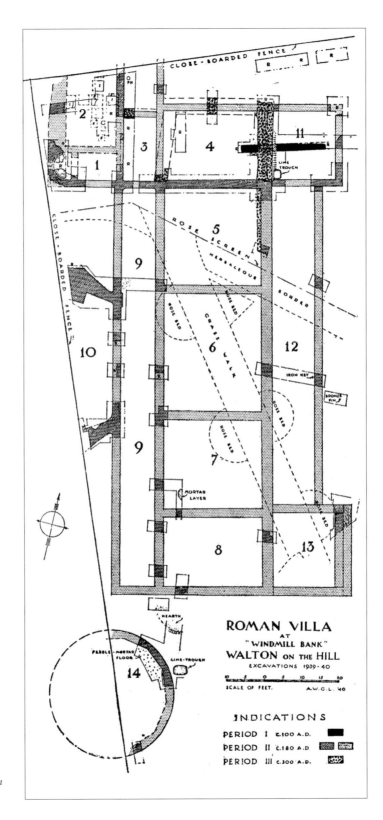

47 Walton on the Hill: villa plan. *From Lowther 1949, fig 1*

going back well into prehistory, but in either case it indicates that villas may have been sited with thought for their setting, and the view to be seen from the house. When we examine Surrey villas in this light it can be seen that there is some support for this suggestion.

Their heights above sea level vary from about 30m (Beddington) to over 200m (Chelsham), with a reasonably even spread in heights between these extremes, but no obvious preference for a lower or higher setting. Almost all are placed on sloping ground; a site actually on a hilltop is rare, apparently only the case at Walton on the Hill. Lowther noted that this villa would have had a particularly fine view to the north; perhaps that explains the choice of site. This is the only Surrey villa known to have an elaborate dining or reception room *(47)*, maybe another indication of an interest in appearance. In the case of the other villas, where the plan is sufficiently well-known it can be seen that the main building is set across the slope, as would be expected. We have a reasonable idea of the direction in which some 13 of the villas faced. A clear majority of these were placed to look generally east or south, two to the north-east, three to the east, two to the south-east and three to the south. Of the other three, two faced west and one north-west. These villas almost invariably face down slope, and if this is accepted as the case with another ten of the probable villas, then the east and south bias is again revealed, although less markedly so: three to the north-east, two to the east and two to the south-east. Of the others, one would face due north and the other two north-west. It is interesting to compare this to the rule for Iron Age round houses, which invariably face east (as do Romano-Celtic temples, probably for the same reason of traditional ritual).

Another clue to the importance of setting is that the villas often seem to be placed almost in defiance of the subsoil. When their placement is examined at a large scale, as already discussed, they can be seen usually to be sited near geological boundaries. Yet at the detailed level they are often found on a clay subsoil when a drier, sandy site could have been chosen nearby. This may be a hint that the view from the villa, or the way it was placed in the landscape, was considered to be more important than the subsoil. More detailed analysis is required of a larger sample before firm conclusions can be drawn. The water supply is another aspect that could be more closely examined in this context. Villas have bath buildings and in some cases ancillary buildings intended for stock. All will have had some animals to water (as well as people of course). A constant and secure water supply will therefore have been of great importance. In many cases it is not difficult to see the likely origin of a villa's supply; for example, Beddington and Carshalton are both close to the Wandle or its tributaries; Abinger is near the Tillingbourne; Farnham and Titsey have streams close by; Rapsley had a nearby spring and some evidence for a line of wooden pipes (in the shape of iron collars) to channel it round to the villa. On the other hand, Walton Heath and Chelsham both seem to be well away from any easily available supply. If these and other sites had to rely on wells, then the implication is that some sort of mechanical aid would be needed to provide a sufficient supply for the bath-house. This suggests again that the location of these villas was chosen for some reason other than an easily available supply of water, even when, as at Walton, the villa itself indicates a wealthy owner.

From what we can see of their plans, most of our villas are modest; there are no certain examples of a larger building complex with integrated wings and courtyards, like Bignor in Sussex. Abinger and Walton Heath are the most likely candidates and it may be significant that they have the best mosaics known in the county. Chiddingfold is a large complex of buildings, but with little sign of a coherent plan, or mosaics. Places like Titsey, Barnwood/Broad Street, Beddington, Farnham and Rapsley all show a modest main building with associated others, not joined in an architectural whole, although buildings tend to be aligned with one another. The area across the north of the Rapsley site was carefully tested and nothing found there. Some intention to impress is shown by the winged corridor villas, whose frontage is usually interpreted as having relatively high projecting side wings with a portico between them. This often hid a less than regular layout behind it, like the Georgian refronting of a medieval timber-framed building. Winged corridor villas probably existed at Beddington, Compton, Walton on the Hill; Titsey (perhaps two), Chelsham, and Rapsley. The last example shows how the effect could be the result of late reordering of an earlier building. A similar sign of 'improvement' through time is suggested by the aisled buildings at places like Titsey, Rapsley and Barnwood, where the simple form, perhaps originally meant as a barn or covered working area, gains extra rooms and even baths. Chiddingfold has a similar aisled building apparently built into the much larger complex. The Titsey building is, however, curious because its aisles were specifically measured at different widths (6 and 8ft (about 1.8 and 2.5m)). It is noticeable that if it had internal partitions in the 'nave' it would be very like Compton which must give cause for thought, especially as we know there was a mosaic (*colour plate 15*). Some of the Rapsley buildings had signs of timber partitions and presumably such things should not be ruled out elsewhere; they would probably not have been noticed by earlier excavators.

Some of the additional buildings were evidently intended for no more than working purposes, with no domestic function, such as the 'barns' at Beddington and the similar timber building at Barnwood. Other small detached buildings may have been intended for ritual use; interpretation of Building 5 at Rapsley as a shrine seems likely enough and others are possible at Walton on the Hill, Titsey and Chiddingfold. None of the sites has produced certain evidence for an associated burial ground, where additional structures might be anticipated. Excavations elsewhere in Britain indicate that they might be several hundred metres distant from the main complex.

Little can be said about the functions of specific rooms, except the baths. Kitchens are sometimes claimed but it seems that they are generally difficult to recognise. The main reception room should be marked by the best mosaic or a room with underfloor heating, and might also be marked by being set between a pair of narrow side rooms. It would normally be expected in the centre of a range of rooms. The Broadstreet Common villa would thus be a good example, again suggesting that we have only a small part of the whole. Walton on the Hill seems to have the only elaborate reception room known in the county.

Baths are known at Rapsley, Chiddingfold (probably), Farnham (both buildings), Compton, Walton on the Hill, Titsey, Bletchingley, Chelsham, Ashtead Common (both buildings), Chatley Farm, and Beddington. They were surely also present at Abinger, Barnwood and Walton Heath (the 'deep pit'). Roman baths were supposed to incorporate a system involving hot, warm and cold rooms. The first two required underfloor heating and a furnace, whose position is of course always an indicator of the location of the hottest room or baths, which will necessarily be immediately next to it. Usually the furnace will have a position for a boiler over it, where the water could be heated. The heated rooms had sub-floors dug to well below the level of unheated rooms. On the sub-floor stacks of tiles were built, placed to take larger tiles which were set on four stacks so that the whole floor area was covered and further layers of cement and the floor covering itself could be laid on them *(53)*. The same system was

48 Walton on the Hill: apsidal plunge bath cut by army practice trenching, 1915. *From Lowther 1949, plate 5*

used for heated rooms not part of the baths, but often here a simpler system with channels under the floor might be used. An example is seen at Farnham in the northern room of the 'house' *(40)*. Heated rooms would also have channels to carry heat up the walls to provide extra heating and draw the heat through from the furnace. These channels were usually made with box flue-tiles; in hot baths particularly, the whole wall might be jacketted in this way. Both hot and cold rooms had plunge baths, which were quite often set into apses, as with the fine example from Walton on the Hill *(47, 48)*.

Compton provides a simple illustration of the classic system, especially if there was a missing room at the south-east corner *(49, 50)*. There could then be an undressing room (*apodyterium*) in the missing wing, a cold room (*frigidarium*) in the area of the corridor marked out as separate by its tiled floor, a warm room (*tepidarium*) in room L with underfloor heating provided by a V-shaped flue, a hot room (*caldarium*) in K and a hot bath in J, both set over tile stacks as shown in the section drawing. The furnace (room I) had cheeks to take the boiler. Rooms J and K were probably originally one room, with continuous box tile jacketting round the walls, partly seen in the photographs *(50)*. When the dividing wall between them was built it was butted up against the tiles. Apparently the stoke hole received repairs at the same time.

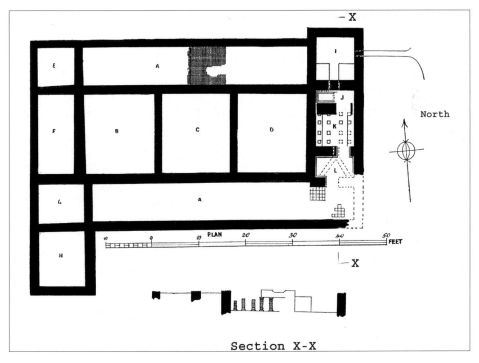

49 Compton: the villa plan. *From Stephenson 1915*

50 Compton: the baths. Top, from the north (note the box tiles in situ, next to the surviving part of the bath); bottom, from the south (note the floor tiles, and the tile stacks in the centre). *From Stephenson 1915, plates 2 and 3*

It is interesting to compare the Farnham bath building *(41)* with the Compton plan. Again we have a walled stoke hole with cheeks on the furnace for a boiler, a narrow room (perhaps a bath rather than Lowther's suggested *sudatorium* or hot steam room), a larger heated room, a warm room and then a cold room and undressing area. The position of the cold plunge bath raises the thought that one could have been lost at Compton projecting eastwards from the corridor. Both sets of baths are otherwise very similar and both are about three metres across. Baths in other villas are less easy to understand and it is probable that the 'proper' system was not always used; no doubt many people were simply grateful for a hot bath. Ashtead has a rare circular heated room, a *laconicum*, which would be more at home in a northern fort *(5, 43)*. It was intended to provide dry heat, but it is difficult to see how it related to the other rooms in the bath-house. At Titsey, room K was interpreted as a kitchen but it had a stokehole and a tiled floor which was probably the base for a hypocaust: it seems to be lower than surrounding floors and the beginnings of tile stacks are hinted at in the 'perspective drawing' *(4)*. This would indicate that the heavily built apse was a cold bath, but the massive construction suggested by the width of the walls and the large stone blocks suggests something more special; could there have been a *nymphaeum*, a water shrine, here, where there is said to be a spring?

The baths made extensive use of a variety of specially-made tiles, and villas in general needed large amounts of roof tiles. These were provided from specialist centres like those described in the next chapter and were often transported many kilometres. Later in the Roman period it seems to have been difficult to find tiles, particularly the more unusual ones, and they were often reused. Thus tile stacks at the Beddington bath-house were mostly roof and flue-tiles rather than the purpose-made *pilae* tiles. The Chatley Farm site had a wide variety of tile and reuse may explain the very curious creation of suspended floors held up by box flue-tiles at Ashtead Common. Our villas and bath-houses mostly use flint or stone rubble for foundations, sometimes with tile or greensand slab bonding-courses above ground level. Rapsley's walls were mostly of pitched stone masonry *(colour plate 4)*. The materials must often have been transported for several kilometres from the chalk or the greensand. It is possible, indeed probable, that often the foundations supported only dwarf walls and the main buildings were timber-framed, but this cannot be demonstrated with certainty. Some sites such as that at Barnwood School had deep foundations capable of supporting complete stone walls, but all the villas had Roman tiled roofs which will have been much heavier than modern ones, and this could account for such foundations, especially on clay. Certainly there is rarely evidence from the sites for enough stone for complete buildings, but as this is Surrey it would usually have been robbed for reuse (consider the case of Chertsey Abbey, much of it used as rubble foundations for Oatlands Palace, itself now vanished; these were both huge buildings). Large scale excavations in Hampshire and Sussex of buildings comparable to the Surrey villas have identified complete walls in collapsed form which in old excavations could easily have been interpreted as rubble or a cobbled surface. Probably therefore there were complete walls in some Surrey buildings, especially in bath-houses.

Little is known of wall decoration as unfortunately it is only possible to list a few sites from which painted plaster has been recovered. Plaster and cement did not survive at Rapsley because of the very acid hillwash. At Beddington a large part of the plaster from a collapsed wall or ceiling was found and hopefully one day a reconstruction of the scheme will be available. It had a pattern of squares and diamonds, red, pink and yellow, with black lines and dots. The Farnham bath had panelled designs with red, yellow and green lines on a white ground. Plaster found at Titsey had colours including red, yellow, green, pink, white, grey and black *(colour plate 15)*. Ashtead is said to have had some wall plaster painted to imitate marble, and some with red and black lines or red and yellow paint splashes. Initial reports suggest that the plaster from the Abinger villa was of high quality.

Red tessellated floors were common in the villas *(colour plate 4)*. They were made from tiles that had failed in the firing process, cut into cubes *(tesserae)*; such 'wasters' could also fire into other colours and one floor at Rapsley was effectively blue. In another room there, a red tessellated floor was divided into squares by lines of some contrasting material, possibly white chalk which had been dissolved by the acid ground conditions. It was laid in Period III, AD 200-220, and retained in part for the rest of the life of the villa. Ironstone pieces were also used as rough tesserae, as at Broadstreet Common and Binscombe. Floor tiles are recorded at Titsey and Compton *(50)* and small bricks laid in a herringbone pattern at Ashtead and Walton Heath. The pink cement called *opus signinum* is known at Compton and Walton on the Hill.

Tessellated pavements needed a good base; the results of a failure to do this can be seen at Rapsley *(colour plate 4)* and in town at Tilly's Lane in Staines *(20)*. At Titsey room E there were small blocks of sandstone with a 'coat' of chalk and over that red tesserae bedded in cement. This accords with the expected method: rammed hard core (or of course the tile base created by a hypocaust), with a finer layer topped with mortar into which the tesserae were pushed while it was still wet. The whole was then levelled. There was obviously only a limited amount of time to set the tesserae; if there was to be a mosaic pattern then it had to be decided and the material prepared in advance. The laying of mosaics was very much a specialist activity.

Only a few mosaic floors are known from the Surrey villas, although we can be sure that more once existed. Tesserae of colours other than red are recorded at Abinger, Chiddingfold, Walton on the Hill, Compton, Beddington, Ashtead and Titsey *(colour plate 15)*, although they may only indicate a blue floor or a simple checkerboard pattern as at Rapsley. The place-name Flore may indicate a long-lost mosaic in the area north of Godstone. As well as the mosaic floor known to have been removed from the Broadstreet Common villa, the corridor there had a coloured rope effect and a small lozenge pattern at one end. Otherwise we have three mosaics, from Walton Heath, Rapsley and Abinger *(colour plates 2, 5, 6)*. It is curious that two out of the three are unusual.

According to Pocock the tesserae of the Walton mosaic included cubes of chalk and broken samian 'upon many of which the portions of figures or ornaments of various kinds occur on the underside'. The description makes it clear that this really was samian pottery, a matter of some interest as the use of samian tesserae in quantity is rare. The very few parallels include the famous 'boy on a dolphin' mosaic at Fishbourne, whose basic scheme (circles and semi-circles) is very like the Walton floor. There are also other parallels between the two mosaics, and they are probably of similar dates (in the second century), so perhaps the same firm was involved. The handles of the central vase in the Walton drawing (a *cantharus*) are shown upside down, which suggests a degree of guesswork, and therefore that this part of the floor was not in good condition when found.

The main mosaic at Rapsley was laid in the principal room of Building 6 as part of the alterations that mark out Period IV. It was placed at the centre of a red tessellated floor and was very poorly preserved; its position can be seen as a darker rectangle on the right-hand edge of *colour plate 4*. The mosaic was a geometric design, with a central square panel surrounded by four octagonal panels joined by four L-shapes. The remaining spaces are filled by lozenges. The design of the central panel is not known, but enough survived of the octagons to show that these had central floral motifs (eight-petalled flowers) surrounded by a guilloche (twisted rope) pattern. The colours were provided by red tile, pale yellow sandstone and buff siltstone. The background is very unusual; it ought to be white tesserae, but in fact is made of *opus signinum*. It is possible that this was a later replacement for chalk tesserae, perhaps damaged by the fire.

The mosaic is dated by excavation to somewhere in the period AD 220-280, and as such is relatively unusual. The Rapsley scheme has parallels elsewhere but with floors of better technical quality dated to the second or fourth centuries, and at widely separated sites. It is therefore not possible to propose strong links with other places at present. It has been suggested that the scheme of the mosaic indicates that it was likely to be laid closer to AD 280 than the earlier part of the date bracket suggested for Period IV at Rapsley, but dating by motifs or layout is not easy as they are long-lasting. For the same reason, the suggested dates for the Walton Heath and Abinger mosaics can only be regarded as probable at present. The latter is octagon-based and likely to be the most common of this type, with three rows of three octagons. Surviving panels have good quality flower motifs and a central cantharus. The floor has quite a lot in common with one from the Bancroft villa in Milton Keynes, which is dated to the early fourth century on archaeological grounds.

Mosaics are presumably a sign of increasing luxury and in general the villa owners seem to have enjoyed a good standard of living, which must have continued over a period of up to 200 years for some sites. They had heated rooms and baths and light (several rough lamps and candlesticks are known at Rapsley), and interior decoration. Some of this was probably intended to impress, like the winged corridor frontages, and this in turn indicates that there were people to impress. Presumably villa owners visited one another and it seems reasonable to assume that they corresponded by letter in the same way as the officers at Vindolanda.

We can say little about who lived in the villas. The buildings and room types (especially baths and heated rooms) imply a 'Roman' way of life, but of course not necessarily Romans as such. It is in fact usually accepted that villa owners were not outsiders but locals making good, perhaps originally tribal aristocracy. There were presumably servants and/or slaves too, although there is no sign of them at Surrey villas; nor do we know where the estate workers lived. The idea of native owners fits well with sites where simple villas develop through time. Some Surrey sites have evidence hinting at Iron Age occupation that might have developed gradually into a villa, but there is no way of knowing that this means that the original occupiers were those who undertook the development. Nor does lack of evidence for previous occupation tell us that this is a venture into new territory; we would not be able to see from archaeology that an earlier site in one location had been abandoned for another one on a different part of the landholding a kilometre away. There were no doubt changes through time in types of ownership, and the way in which Iron Age systems changed into Roman-recognised ones is not really understood. The case of Julius Bellicus makes it clear that landholding as we would recognise it was in existence by the second century, and later Roman landowners are known to have owned estates all over the Empire including in Britain. It would probably be impossible to distinguish between privately-owned small villas and places run by stewards. We also have no way of telling if it was common for owners to move between town and country on a regular basis. Some of the sites imply that there may be expanding family groups; this seems the best explanation for a site like Titsey, where there are two facing villas close together. Other sites like Rapsley and Ashtead have similar evidence. If the interpretation is correct then again it supports the idea of gradual development over the centuries, matching how most villas themselves grew incrementally.

There are some hints of possible outsiders: for example Abinger and Walton Heath seem to be well-appointed from early on, although this need imply no more than high-ranking local Britons. Ashtead is perhaps a more likely case, built by an ex-military man, although even he could be retiring to his homeland of course. He seems to have been someone who knew about making tiles but did not entirely understand heating systems. A military

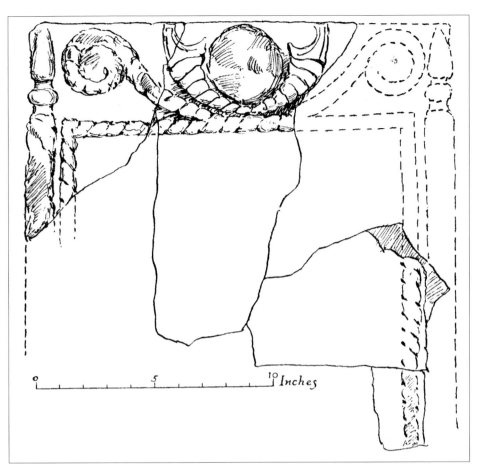

51 Ashtead Common: fragments of decorated sandstone slab. *From Lowther 1930, fig 11*

connection is perhaps suggested by the circular laconicum and by stone fragments found at the site which probably had a painted inscription *(51)*. The Ashtead buildings and tiles have an air of experimentation. One room had underfloor heating made by laying box tiles as flues (a system which has something of a parallel at the Holt legionary tileworks near Chester); another living room had its walls completely jacketted by box flue-tiles *(52)* when this would only be expected in a bath-house. This jacketting was taken right down to the base of the sub-floor when it would be usual to stop at the main floor level, to allow access for the hot air (as shown in *53*). As a result tiles had to be made with special cut-outs. Some box tiles were made with 'fish tails' sticking out at the back for bonding into the wall, which probably did not work very well and would have been very difficult to transport.

The house *(44)* has a unique plan with some awkwardly-shaped rooms and rather too much heating. It is large and was apparently well-floored with

52 Ashtead Common: contemporary photograph of work in progress on Room 6. Stacks of *pilae* tiles can be seen and the box flue-tile jacketting of two of the walls. *Courtesy Leatherhead Museum*

various forms of tile including herringbone-pattern bricks, and originally had a well-appointed separate bath-house. It may even have had window glass along the lengthy front corridor and engaged columns made from quarter and semi-circular tiles. It is the only Surrey site where gold jewellery has been found (a hollow cone earring and piece of gold chain). The evidence overall suggests considerable expense at an unpromising location: sticky clay, right next door to an operating tileworks. It is reasonable to conclude that we have here a self-made man living with his business. We may know something of his name from the letters on one of his products, the 'dog and stag' tiles *(colour plate 8)*: G I S and I V FE. It is possible that they refer to the owner of the tilery and his manager, perhaps G[aius] I[ulius] S[...] and I[ulius] V[...] FE[cit] (that is, Iulius V... made this). If this is correct it suggests a Roman citizen owner (because he has the *tria nomina*, three names) and his freedman.

EIGHT

INDUSTRY

Surrey has little in the way of special natural resources. There is iron ore in places but of poor grade; the Roman-period Wealden iron industry was further south, in Sussex. There is no good quality building stone. The Greensand produces both soft and hard material; the soft can be easily shaped but is too readily eroded by weather action to be of much value and the hard is usually too hard to be worked into ashlar blocks, and not suitably layered. There is little evidence for use of the softer material in the Roman period, but the harder was used in rubble foundations and as quoins or as rough levelling courses in flint walls. It is however of considerable interest that Reigate stone has been identified in use in Southwark in pre-Boudican buildings. Perhaps it was one of the first stone sources to have been discovered near London. It does not seem to be used there much later on, which suggests that it was quickly found to be inferior to stone from more distant places.

The flint, chalk and greensand used in Surrey villas must have come from quarries on the Downs and in the Lower Greensand. Rosamond Hanworth has suggested that the villa at Rapsley had a sandstone quarry at Pitch Hill on its estate because good quality ashlar was used in foundations and drains, and this may have been the source of some of the stone used at other Surrey sites. Only a careful programme of scientific analysis will make it possible to trace the sources of stone for the Surrey villas and thereby allow us to consider if there were one or two quarries supplying most sites or if it was more common for each villa to use resources from its own estate. The evidence of tile supply (see below) suggests that it is quite reasonable to postulate quarries run on a semi-industrial basis, supplying sites over considerable distances. If the Rapsley estate also included the Wykehurst tile kiln, and areas of woodland, then it could have supplied a wide range of building material.

Surrey abounds in clay and fast growing trees *(29, colour plate 1)*, and as a result the countryside in the Roman period has the county's first identifiable industry, if by industry we understand something more than craftsmen producing items generally for local use. This can certainly be demonstrated for the clays, because we know some of the kiln sites where clay was fired to make pottery and tiles and we can find the products. Roman-style buildings required tiles in a number of guises and often in considerable quantity and these are known to have been produced at sites near Ashtead, Reigate and Cranleigh. Thus all three of the main Surrey clay types were used: London Clay, Gault Clay and Weald Clay. Tiles were required especially for roofs and for bath buildings and other rooms that required heating. Roofs needed *tegulae* and *imbrices*, which were heavy: it has been calculated that an area say 5m by 3m would weigh over a ton. The *tegula* was flat with raised side flanges and the *imbrex* was curved to cover the adjoining flanges of two *tegulae*, giving the well-known corrugated effect. The tiles overlapped from top to bottom but it is not clear how the ridge was covered. Complex pots in tile fabric have sometimes been interpreted as chimney pots, but most are likely to have been intended for a ritual use *(68)*. Heating systems needed different sized tiles for raised floors and box flues to form channels up the walls *(53)*, and sometimes wedge-shaped

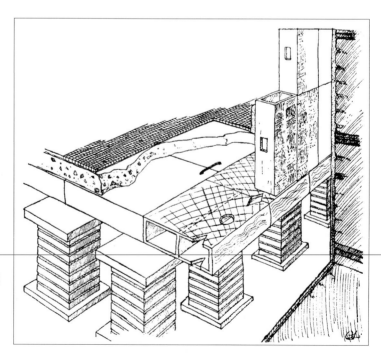

53 A possible use for the double box flue-tiles found at Ashtead Common, showing also the way the hypocaust floor was raised and how box flue-tiles could jacket a wall. *From Lowther 1930, fig 12*

voussoirs to make lightweight curved ceilings. Tiles were also produced for floor coverings and cut up for tesserae.

Like modern bricks Roman tiles could be used in all sorts of ways, even when broken, and will last for a long time. This may be one reason why tile making seems to have been much less common later in the Roman period, when there is clear evidence for reuse of tile. This raises the interesting picture of Roman builders dismantling buildings and carefully keeping reusable tiles just like workmen cleaning old bricks today. Tiles were used for other purposes such as drains, hearths and as covers over burials, and this, together with their constant reuse, means that the discovery of tile debris should be treated with care and not taken to be certain evidence for a high-status building, or act as a good guide to date (they could even be reused in later centuries).

Tiles were made by specialists, who must originally have come from within the Empire. There are hints that some makers learnt their trade in or perhaps with the army. Given the weight of tiles, logic would have the tile kilns placed as near as possible to where tiles were required, but known kilns are often well away from the towns one would think would be the largest market. The Ashtead Common tileworks is located quite close to Stane Street but it is not obvious why this particular site was chosen. Evidence for this centre was recognised by Lowther in the 1920s in the shape of an extensive spread of burnt material (red-fired clay and black soil with charcoal fragments) and fragments of tile 'wasters' (tiles warped or broken in the firing process). Subsequent excavations by John Hampton in the 1960s examined some of the complicated remains of the kilns and associated debris, leading to the conclusion that the tiles had been made in 'clamps', that is, effectively in covered bonfires. Wasters were found that confirmed production of certain types of tile at the site. These were the usual tiles for roofs and hypocaust systems, small tiles for herringbone pattern floors, and quarter and semi-circular tiles to make columns. Rare double box flue-tiles were made (their suggested use is shown in *53*). Associated pottery and other evidence suggests that the tilery was in production in the second century.

John Hampton also plotted clay pits near the villa, one probably seventeenth century in date but the other almost certainly Roman *(54)*. This pit was roughly triangular with sides about 87 yards (80m) long, 6 feet (say 2m) deep at its deepest point. Three possible kilns (A, B and C) were identified on the edges of the quarry; Hampton suggests that these would have been the latest in use, others having been destroyed as the quarry expanded. He also found the corner of an enclosure wall or new building *(55)* and recorded shallow clay pits south-west of the villa. These were suggested to be the source of the material for the tiles used in the villa's first construction. Hampton was able to calculate, allowing for considerable wastage in the production process, that enough clay had been won to produce tiles to roof 50 villas of the size of Ashtead, as well as the more unusual tiles.

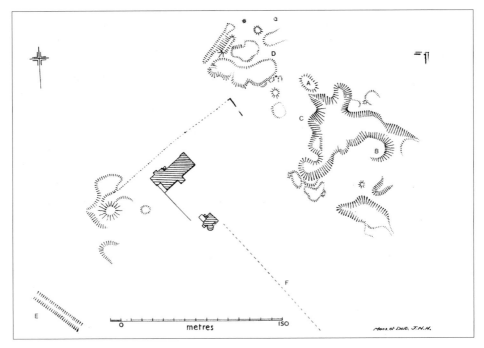

54 Ashtead Common: plan of the clay pits and their relationship to the villa. A, B and C are kilns on the edge of the Roman clay pit; D marks probably seventeenth century clay pits; E is a nearby earthwork of unknown date and F is the Roman road connecting the site to Stane Street. The broken line north of the villa marks a possible enclosure wall, whose corner is shown on *55*. *Drawing: John Hampton*

A brick-built tile kiln is known from a record made during building works in 1922 at the former West Park Asylum site at Horton, near Epsom; it is not far from Ashtead Common and so may be part of the same industry. If so, it is interesting that a formal kiln, rather than a tile clamp, was being used; perhaps a different date is implied. There is a better-studied example of such a kiln (although it differs in a number of details) at Wykehurst Farm near Ewhurst, where traces of the associated workshop were also found in excavations by Goodchild in 1936. The site is near the branch road from Alfoldean to Farley Heath and near enough to Rapsley to have been on the villa's estate; it was perhaps intended to supply both the villa and the roadside settlement.

The Wykehurst kiln *(56)* was constructed of tiles which are thought to have been made on the site in a tile clamp. It was made by digging out a large rectangular hole, lining it with tiles and clay, and making an arrangement of a central flue and seven cross flues by tile-built walls corbelled across the central flue. The spaces between the walls acted as the cross flues and these were covered by tiles and clay to form an oven floor nearly 9ft 2in (nearly 3m) square). Gaps were left in the floor to allow for the circulation of heat, which came from a fire served by a large sunken stokehole. The latter was provided with a drain made of curved roof tiles, perhaps significantly like the drains at Rapsley. Tiles were made and allowed to dry to a leather-hard state and then stacked on edge on the oven floor, where they were surrounded by a temporary roof and walls made of clay blocks. After firing these blocks were removed and the fired tiles were recovered. The process would have created many wasters, which were broken up and used to make a wide paved area to one side of the kiln, probably to act as a place to dry the newly-made tiles before they were fired. It also served as a working area for the creation of tile tesserae about 1 inch (25mm) square which were made from the wasters; red, blue and brown being possible because of the effects of differential firing. No drying sheds were found but only a small part of the paved area was excavated properly and they are likely to have existed.

The Wykehurst kiln produced the standard roof tiles, but also a very unusual type, pear-shaped with a flat top which was pierced for a nail (57). It seems to have been intended as a clay tile equivalent of a stone diamond-shaped roof slab. As such it is apparently paralleled only by a heptagonal tile type from one other

55 Ashtead Common: corner of enclosure wall or building, near the kilns. *Photograph: John Hampton*

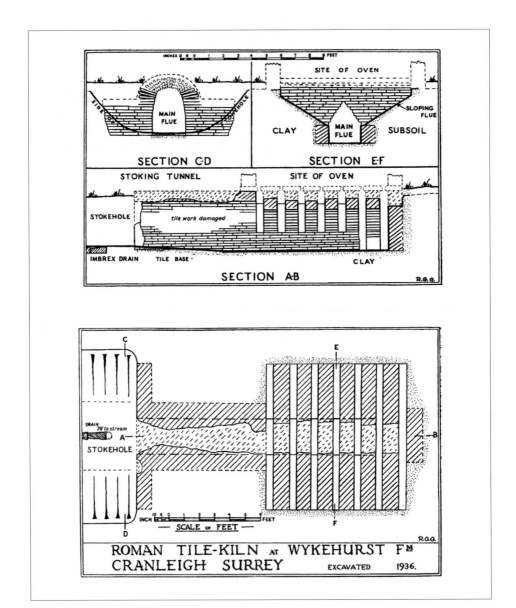

56 Plan and sections of the tile kiln at Wykehurst Farm. *From Goodchild 1937, figs 4 and 5*

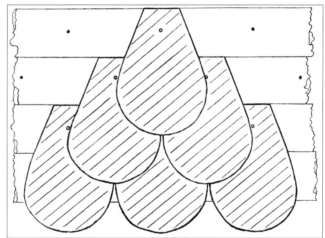

57 Roman pear-shaped tile from Rapsley, and a suggested method for its original intended use. *From Hanworth 1968, plate 1 and Goodchild 1937, fig 7*

site in Britain. There is one pear-shaped tile from Rapsley which was evidently used as a base for a doorpost; no others were found there and it seems that the site for which they were intended has yet to be discovered. Presumably they were prepared for a special order. Wykehurst also produced box flue-tiles with a combed pattern, other standard building tiles, the tesserae already noted and semi-circular tiles (with a 9in (230mm) diameter) intended to be used in the creation of attached columns similar to those at the Ashtead villa. If the Rapsley tile with the sheep print on it *(35)* came from Wykehurst, then it may imply that the tiler was also a part-time farmer. Another tile at Rapsley had letters on it written pre-firing: EP. FRAB. VMAN; their meaning is unknown but they suggest a degree of literacy.

A tilery has long been suspected at Doods Farm near Reigate and recent excavations have put the matter beyond doubt with the discovery of tile-manufacturing debris. It remains to be seen if this tilery is also associated with a villa; there is a hint of Roman occupation on a nearby site. Tiles in the Reigate fabric have been traced on many London sites, usually in small quantities except for the Billingsgate bath-house, which presumably was a major contract. Products included box flue-tiles and have been found as far afield as Canterbury. The London site information suggests a mid–late second century date for this tileworks.

Box tiles from Reigate and Ashtead were decorated with patterns produced by using a roller stamp on the clay before it was fired, which for some patterns at least covered half of the face of a box tile; examples from Ashtead show cases where the registration was less than exact *(colour plate 9)*. In fact this would not have mattered, as the purpose of the pattern was to provide a key for wall plaster. This did not stop the makers indulging a flair for artistry, the finest example perhaps being the well-known 'dog and stag' pattern tiles made at Ashtead *(colour plate 8)*. It may be that the patterns acted as a mark of quality (real or supposed). They were first studied in depth by Lowther following his excavations at Ashtead, and his corpus was published by Surrey Archaeological Society in 1948. It has recently been substantially updated by Ian Betts, Ernest Black and John Gower. Dies were given numbers and more than 100 are now recognised, although many are similar. Six are known from Ashtead itself: dies 1, 4, 5, 6, 14, and 66 *(58)*. Two of these (1 and 66) were certainly made at the site as wasters have been found; it is likely that the others were as well. Dies 4 and 5 have very similar chevron patterns to die 66. Die 5 was apparently also used at Reigate.

Study of sites at which the patterns have been found yields interesting results. Although dies 1 and 66 were made at Ashtead they are probably not represented in the villa or bath house; nor are they seen at the Roman building site at Ashtead Church. This tends to confirm that the tiles found there were robbed from the Ashtead buildings for reuse in the late Roman period, as Lowther thought. There is probably a chronological implication: the kilns studied by Hampton are likely to have been the last in operation, which suggests that dies 1 and 66 were the last in use there and that the dies found in the villa were used on earlier products. Production was probably mostly in the second century but the way tiles last and were often reused makes them difficult to date precisely. Pottery associated with Hampton's part of the tileworks suggests that the later production was perhaps in the middle of the second century. The associations of the Reigate-produced die 5 tiles suggests that these are to be dated mid–late second century, which may indicate that the tiler moved there after Ashtead. Die 5 is used at Ashtead itself in the baths added later to the villa, so presumably could be a late product.

The distribution of tiles with Ashtead dies is impressive: sites in Surrey include the two Walton villas, Ewell and Beddington; in Sussex, Fishbourne, Chichester and Alfoldean; there are sites in London and as far afield as

58 The main patterns used on relief-patterned tiles in Surrey. *Drawing author, after Betts et al 1994, 74, 75, 85 and 124*

Canterbury, Chelmsford and St Albans. It is interesting that there seems to be no link with Silchester. All the Ashtead products are represented at London and at Verulamium, the last with the exception of die 6 (dog and stag), which is not widely found but curiously turns up at Chelmsford in Essex. Dies 4, 5, and 66 are seen at Alfoldean. Only a few Surrey sites received patterned box tiles from anywhere other than Ashtead. There is very little link with the Southwark sites, and the Chatley Farm bath-house has only one of the Ashtead products (see further above). Dorking, Staines and Croydon have single non-Ashtead dies and Beddington and Rapsley have tiles from sites in Sussex.

The far-flung distribution of Ashtead patterns has led some to suggest secondary production centres using the same roller stamp, but as scientific analysis has shown that Reigate products reached Canterbury it does not seem unreasonable to accept that Ashtead products could travel as far. The products of the Alice Holt/Farnham pottery industry provided a major part of London's supply of coarse pottery although it would have been perfectly possible to manufacture pottery much closer to the city. We should accept that sources of supply were affected by factors other than simple economics. It is also note-worthy that London's supply of box flue-tiles seems to have come from further out than most of its regular tile supply in the first and second centuries. Perhaps these specialist products were being made for local use in villas and the oppor-tunity was taken to sell some also to the towns. Similarly the products of a kiln very like the Wykehurst Farm example, at Hartfield just over the border in Sussex and close to the London–Lewes road, are known to have reached villas at Beddington and Beddingham, probably more than 30km away to north and south respectively *(17)*. Documentary evidence provides an interesting medieval parallel: in 1372/3 a hall roof at Banstead received 10,500 tiles from Ashtead and 10,000 from Reigate, with two special crest tiles from Cheam.

The other main industry was the manufacture of pottery. A number of pottery kilns are known in the county but except on the western border they were evidently only small-scale producers, presumably filling a local need. One or two kilns are known at Farley Heath *(colour plate 13)*; an early drawing is supposed to show a kiln with its last load of complete pots still in situ, although it is a very curious shape. Perhaps pots were produced for use at the temple site. Other small-scale production is possible at Wisley and Ashtead (where finds include pottery wasters), and there are supposed to be Roman predeces-sors of the medieval kilns in the Limpsfield area, but the evidence is rather weak. The Staines region has been suggested as the centre for the production of early fine wares around AD 70-120: green-glazed and possibly also mica-dusted vessels, often copying samian forms. The distribution, however, seems to be nearly all north and east of Staines so it is perhaps more likely that the production centre was further away.

Almost all fine wares in Roman Surrey came from outside the county but much of its coarse pottery was supplied by the Alice Holt/Farnham industry.

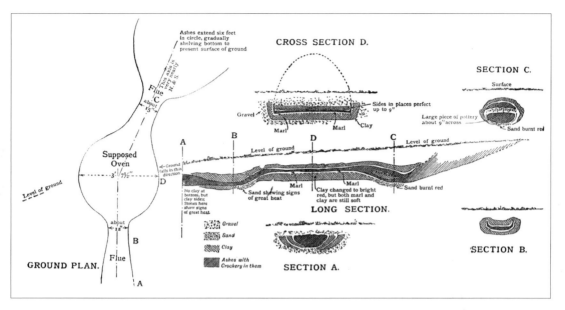

59 Early twentieth-century drawing of double-flue pottery kiln from near Farnham. *From Falkner 1907, 230*

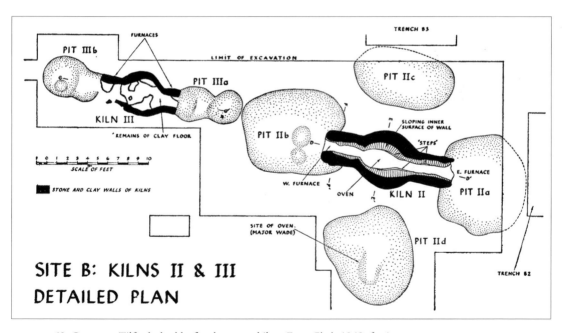

60 Overwey, Tilford: double-flued pottery kilns. *From Clark 1949, fig 4*

It is often just referred to as Alice Holt but it is clear that much evidence has been lost across the Farnham area and the industry had outliers as far east as Tilford. It started early in the Roman period and in the first and early second century it was a major supplier to Surrey and the London area as well as further afield. Following a decline in the later second to later third centuries the industry became one of Roman Britain's largest pottery producers, supplying a wide area of the South-East, including a high percentage of London's coarse pottery requirements. Pottery was produced to standard shapes and sizes, so there was obviously a form of control over production.

Several kilns are known, of an unusual type. The architect Harold Falkner drew one found near Farnham in 1905, a very fine record for its day *(59)*. Another discovered at Snailslynch in 1928 supposedly had the last load still in position. The kilns have been best studied by Tony Clark, at Overwey near Tilford, where three kilns were found in excavation in 1947-8 *(60)*. They were sunk deliberately into the ground; sandstone was used among the furnace lining material but only clay was used to line the ovens themselves. There were signs that the kilns had been refloored. They were the first examples of double-flued kilns to be properly understood; each had two stokeholes and no oven floor. Clark suggested that the two furnaces were needed to give even firing as there was no oven floor to allow heat to travel to the back of the kiln. Pots were stacked directly on the floor of the kiln and then the ovens had domes formed over them with clay and straw (large pieces were found in the excavation). After each firing the domes were broken off so that the pots could be removed. Clark argued that the kilns were only in production for a short period of time, perhaps for about five years from about AD 363 to 368.

The Alice Holt/Farnham industry produced pottery for cooking and everyday storage requirements, generally grey wares, sometimes with simple white or grey slip, burnishing or incised decoration *(61)*. Some of the pots from the Overwey kilns are known as Portchester D ware but they are obviously related to the wider industry's products. Several of the fragments recorded on the beautiful drawings of finds from Leveson Gower's excavation at Titsey are from Overwey or more generally Alice Holt/Farnham products *(colour plate 16)*. A selection of Overwey products is shown in the drawing *(62)*. Top left is a distinctive Farnham area storage jar made in small numbers at Overwey (see also the large fragment on *61*). Below that are two jars, the lower of which was made in large numbers; and below again is a very typical flanged bowl (see also *colour plate 16*, I, IV, XXVI). At the top right are various dishes, the top two in particular being very common. Below them are a flagon (see also *61*) and a strainer, perhaps for use in making cheese (see also *colour plate 16*, XXII). Finally, at the bottom right, are three jars, showing how this common form was made in several useful sizes. Mention should also be made of the very large storage jars up to 650mm in height produced by the Alice Holt/Farnham industry. It can be seen that consumers had a good range of products available to them.

61 Fragments of three vessels from the Overwey kilns. Top left, flagon; top right, jar; bottom, large storage jar. *Photograph: Brian Wood, courtesy Surrey Archaeological Society and Guildford Museum*

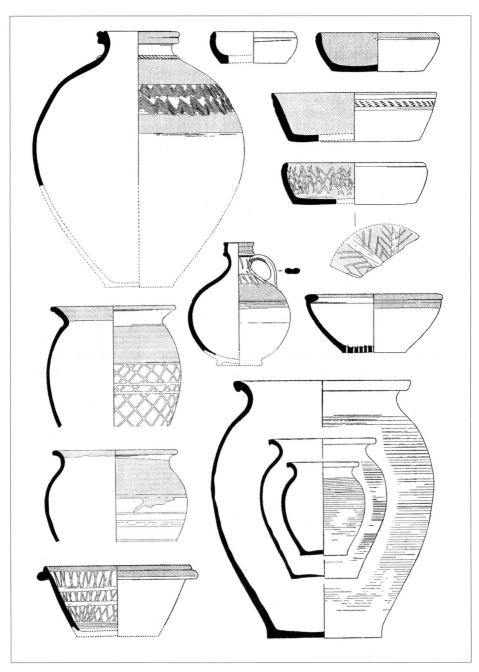

62 Pottery from the Overwey kilns. The shading represents white slip. A variety of types for household use: jars, dishes, a bowl, a flagon and a strainer. Height of flagon: 164mm. *Drawing: author, after Clark 1949, figs 6-9*

NINE

BURIALS AND BELIEFS

Religious beliefs spring from the sense of there being major powers outside human control and also from the consciousness that human life is finite. As a result rituals develop associated with life and death. Recent work in Surrey has contributed a wealth of new information for the Roman period: the temple site at Wanborough; new excavations at the Farley Heath temple and fresh study of the finds; evidence suggestive of ritual at Frensham, Westcott, Betchworth and perhaps Godstone; new interpretations at Ewell and Chiddingfold. As this is being written excavations are continuing at a newly discovered temple site in Southwark. There is more burial evidence, particularly from Southwark, but also from Staines, at last confirming the location of one cemetery there.

It is obviously difficult for anyone to understand properly another person's religious beliefs, and even more so when looking back into the past. For instance, people brought up in the western rational tradition find it hard to understand how other peoples might react to shamans. On the other hand in the modern western world it is apparently possible for some people to take horoscopes seriously. Even in the Roman Empire one person's religion could be regarded by another as superstition. Intensity of belief will have varied from individual to individual then as now. There are also difficulties with the interpretation of archaeological finds. Those that cannot be explained may be interpreted as ritual objects when they actually had some more mundane purpose – even perhaps as toys. Alternatively, we may not recognise finds and features that actually did have a ritual purpose. Roman period ritual activity often involved the burial of objects; when archaeologists find complete objects it is always likely to be because they were deliberately placed below the ground surface. Burials were often accompanied by grave goods, sometimes perhaps because the corpse was dressed as in life (dress fittings, personal ornaments like hairpins or jewellery), or to provide comfort in the afterlife, for example perfume bottles, flagons, lamps, all perhaps full. Objects were sometimes old and worn, even deliberately broken as a ritual of dedication (perhaps making them dead too). Similar dedications were made at temple and other ritual sites.

Relatively few burials are known from Roman Surrey as a whole, which is unfortunate as it is the most immediate way to know more about the people themselves. There are also no surviving burial inscriptions, the result of being in an area where there is no good local source of suitable stone. It was therefore either too expensive to import or too valuable not to reuse later; it is possible that wooden inscriptions were used. As a general rule, burials in the first part of the Roman period were cremations, and in the second, inhumations, yet another example of a change between early and late Roman Britain. Either might be marked by finds of complete pots, used as containers for cremated bones or as accessory vessels. The rule was that burials should be outside the settlement area, except for babies (some are noted in Staines, for instance). It is particularly noticeable in towns where usually burials line the roads leaving the settlements.

This can now be seen in Southwark and Staines but the evidence is less clear for the other roadside settlements. In Ewell, Croydon and north Kingston there is some evidence for inhumations but here and at Staines the situation is complicated by known or possible Saxon burials; on the other hand cremation urns possibly associated with the Kingston Hill settlement might be Bronze Age. There are certainly Roman lead coffins from Croydon (interestingly only one is known from Southwark) which ought to indicate high-status burials, and a very late burial next to a Saxon burial ground, which perhaps suggests that the latter was continuing and extending an earlier cemetery. In Ewell, inhumations south of the settlement near Stane Street seem to be Saxon, but they are in the right area for Roman burials so again there may be a degree of overlap. Finds of coins and complete pots suggest that there were cremations around the Bourne Hall area, and Diamond noted that there were burials near the ritual shafts. He also recorded a nearby mound that he took to be a Roman-period barrow, which is possible, in contrast to a second noted in the Glyn House grounds which is surely too close to the centre of the settlement. Another possible Roman barrow is recorded at Morden, near Merton, which makes it noteworthy that one is also known near Pulborough in Sussex, suggesting a kind of Stane Street-related distribution. They were of course intended to be prominent in the landscape.

The increasing evidence for burials in Southwark includes a newly discovered cemetery at America Street, which adds to the burials known from within the two main islands, suggesting that the formal settlement would not have covered all of their surface area. The cemetery was on the north-western tip of the south island; it had over 150 inhumations, which intercut showing that there were different phases. Burials were accompanied by personal ornaments including necklaces, bracelets and rings. There were at least four coffins packed with lime, presumably in an attempt to preserve the body, matching similar evidence found elsewhere in Southwark. Some fourth century inhumation burials have been found within the former inhabited area, which indicates contraction of the settlement. For example 14 burials were found on the 15-23 Southwark Street site (the possible *mansio*), cut into earlier buildings.

Southwark's main burial area seems to have been south of the islands, in and around the triangle formed by the junction of Stane Street and Watling Street. The evidence is often limited but it does appear all over the area, and early records note urns and burnt bones in quantity, so no doubt much has been lost over the years. Burials include an unusually early inhumation from Harper Road. Sometimes more than burial ritual is indicated: one of a large group of wells in Swan Street (near the northern part of the triangle) contained a human skeleton *(71)*. This and other wells had finds indicating ritual deposits. They might even have been dug for this reason: the Tabard Square temples are not far away.

Not far to the east, in Great Dover Street *(18, 63)*, a group of small structures is our first evidence for high-status burials alongside a main road (in this case Watling Street), being added to over the years and presumably therefore marking family burial plots (and perhaps also their clients or servants). There were burials here from about AD 120 to the end of the fourth century, some 26 inhumations and eight cremations being found. The latter included a *bustum*, in which a rectangular pit is dug and the cremation pyre built above it; eventually all the burnt material is scraped into the pit with perhaps additional offerings. The Great Dover Street *bustum* gained a fleeting notoriety as a

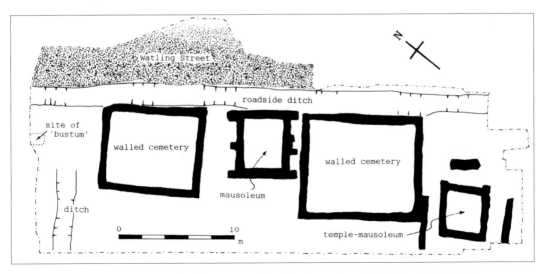

63 Great Dover Street, Southwark: cemetery plan. *Drawing: author, after Sheldon 2000, fig 8.6*

64 Samian ware bowl (about AD 70-90) probably from a burial, London Road, Staines.
Photograph: author

supposed female gladiator, a suggestion derived from the decoration on the eight accompanying lamps, but their imagery was appropriate to a normal burial. There were also six tazze (small frilled-edge dishes on integral stands), normally used as censers. Further east along Watling Street early records mention finds of Roman glass vessels from Peckham High Street, which should indicate burials, but it is just too far away to be linked to Southwark and so presumably indicates a nearby settlement, south of the main road.

Burial evidence around Staines continues to be very limited. Its likely location along roads raises the interesting possibility that there was a cemetery on the island to the north-west. The location of the parish church on this island is then noteworthy, hinting at a possible origin as a *martyrium* (the real or supposed burial site of a Christian martyr), but clearly proper evidence is required before this can be taken further. To the east of the town there are early imprecise references to several groups of complete pots and a 3in (80mm) high glass 'ampulla' which are likely to indicate burials. Recent excavations at the Old Police Station site located ditches parallel to and at right angles to the Roman road to London, with fills containing a lot of pottery. There was evidence for burials: two inhumations, one radiocarbon dated to between AD 70 and 130, and three definite and two possible cremations. A more or less complete samian bowl from the site had probably once furnished a burial, perhaps as an accessory vessel. It is likely to have been carefully chosen for its ceremonial procession; for burials, torches would be appropriate even in daylight *(64)*. This site also produced a probably first-century iron spearhead. A little further along London Road more inhumations have been found but they are thought mostly to be in a later Saxon execution cemetery. Some may be Roman, to judge from their hobnailed boots *(22)*.

One of the cremations at the Old Police Station site was possibly a *bustum*. The Staines pit held lots of burnt material including human bone, but as at Southwark, the sides of the pit were not burnt and the fill included unburnt grave goods *(15, 65)*. These included two fine disc brooches with traces of the chain that once held them together, two glass perfume flasks, a fine glass dish, a complete small samian dish, fragments of a once complete flagon and other

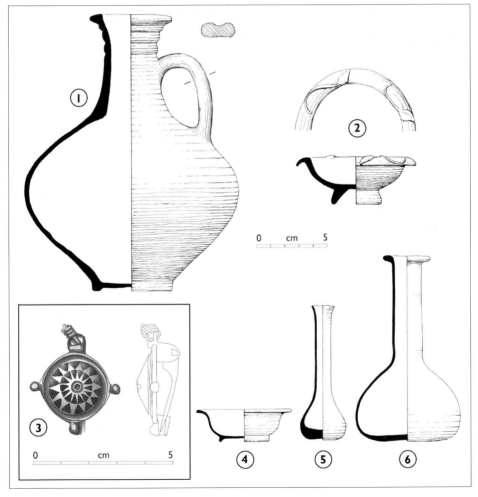

65 Finds from the Staines *bustum*. 1: Verulamium region flagon; 2: samian dish; 3: enameled disc brooch, one of a pair; 4-6: glass dish and phials. *Courtesy Surrey County Archaeological Unit*

material such as about 60 nails, perhaps from the pyre structure. The finds suggest a mid to late second-century date, although a possibly associated coin dated to the late third or early fourth century would have to be regarded as intrusive in that case. This would be rather late for a cremation but it is not impossible that the grave goods were old cherished heirlooms by the time of their eventual burial. A nearby inurned cremation was in a pot of similar date to the coin, and there are other late examples.

Burial evidence from the countryside is limited in what it can tell us as it has rarely been well recorded. It is mostly early notes of complete pottery vessels, with few details other than about the pots themselves. Presumably the burials were near settlements but it is rarely possible to see a link; the most likely seems to be at Charterhouse School, where a cemetery is known a few hundred metres from a contemporary occupation site. Likely cremation burials plotted north of Farley Heath form an interesting line that perhaps hints at the course of a road. One group from a steeply-sloping site near the temple included a pot with a very elaborate lead repair, shaped round much of the interior of the base. Recent discoveries include shallow scoops apparently containing cremations at Farleigh Court (near Chelsham) and Barnwood School; if they are typical it is not surprising that so many burials have gone unnoticed over the years. Pottery vessels from cremation cemeteries at Tilford, Charterhouse and Haslemere are dated to the late Iron Age into the earlier Roman period and indicate the possibility of continuity of settlement. There are various other examples of cremations singly or in groups, as for example at Wotton and near Merrow. This last find is typical: an early discovery during 'trenching and digging' of up to 12 whole pots and several others in fragments, with evidence noted for cremations. Some of the pots seem surprisingly late for cremation burials, but there is nothing to suggest that they were accompanying inhumations. This find hints at the presence of quite a large settlement, although, as so often, nothing relevant is known. The lateness of the cremations is interesting as it seems quite common and may explain the rarity of inhumations in the countryside: perhaps it took a long time for the new fashion to catch on. Unaccompanied burials are of course difficult to date without some technique such as radiocarbon dating, which was used recently to show that two inhumations found between Staines and Laleham were of the Roman period.

Two finds provide a little more detail. About 2km to the south-east of Ewell a site known as The Looe produced evidence for the cremation burial of a male in a late first or early second-century pot inserted into the fill of an earlier large pit, with a dog buried nearby. There was a ritual element in the backfilling of the pit and two others nearby which presumably influenced the location of the burial. As well as burnt bone, the pot's fill included four nails and three bone gaming counters. Five more counters were found face down under the pot and a ninth 2ft (61cm) away *(72)*. The second find was not far south of Beddington, at Bandon Hill, curiously enough in a modern cemetery. Finds in grave digging included a large hand-made jar full of partly burnt human bone and a single bent nail. It was probably of third century date but may have been accompanied by a small grey ware beaker dated about AD 100-130, which was worn and probably old when buried, and a single-handled flagon probably of the second half of the third century. The other two vessels were found sufficiently far away to be possibly from another burial and in fact two years later (1976) two more probable burial jars were found, with more accessory vessels, again with wide-ranging dates.

Each of the villas must have had a related cemetery but none is known; only at Beddington can one be postulated from the discovery of coffins nearby. They were found at the church on the other side of the river but are unlikely to have been moved there after the Roman period. The site might have been felt suitable by the villa's owners. A similar situation is possible at Abinger as well, while at Walton on the Hill it may be that the adjoining circular building was a mausoleum or temple-mausoleum. A bronze face mask *(69)* found about 200 yards from the Titsey villa may also be relevant to this discussion, as it has been suggested that it was a box fitting that would have been appropriate for a funerary or ritual purpose. Two coffins have been found at Beddington, a lead one, discovered about 1870 *(66)*, and one of stone, found in 1930. This was made of an Oolitic limestone which probably came from northern England or northern France; oddly enough northern French Oolite was noted at the

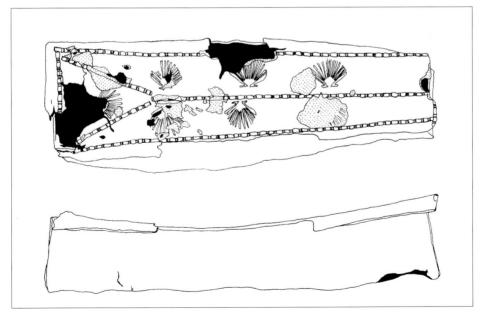

66 Lead coffin from Beddington church. *Drawing: author, after Adkins and Adkins 1984, fig 1*

Titsey temple. The Beddington coffin weighed about two tons, which raises interesting questions about the difficulties of transport and the mechanics of lowering it into the grave. Its contents were not well recorded: supposedly a tall female skeleton with three glass vessels. Lead coffins are not common and presumably indicate high status, so it would be appropriate to note an early record of one other find: a lead coffin with scallop shell ornament and a skeleton, with three other skeletons nearby, from Battersea Fields (now Recreation Ground).

We can be sure that for most people in early Roman Surrey, religious beliefs and burial rituals will have developed from those already in existence in the preceding periods, and would have been focussed on the natural world, including aspects of the heavens such as sun and moon, thunder and lightning. Particular places had their own spirits: a hill top, a spring, a river or marshy place, a tree or grove, under the ground. Home and hearth, extended to settlement and thus on up to a whole locality or one's own tribal group (in some ways perhaps the same thing) were also very important. These concepts were personified as deities who might be seen as having particular attributes exemplified by animals such as the bull, ram, dog or raven or objects such as the wheel or the axe. Their aid and protection were sought with the problems of daily life.

At present we cannot say if the sites that came to have temples or other indications of religious significance in the Roman period were already sacred in prehistory, but there are some indications that this was often the case. The difficulty is that usually the nature of earlier finds (and structures if any) is rarely sufficient on its own to establish that the site was used for ritual. The picture is further complicated by the undoubted evidence for Roman-period deposition of certain prehistoric artefacts at sacred sites, objects such as Neolithic polished axes or Bronze Age weapons. Thus the finds of prehistoric axes at places like Farley Heath may represent Roman-period rather than prehistoric offerings. Similarly, finds of Iron Age coins may indicate pre-Roman activity, but the thousands of Iron Age coins found at Wanborough are thought to have been placed at the site in the early Roman period. It is therefore possible that this may also be true for the much smaller numbers discovered at Farley Heath, Frensham and Godstone, if the last site is relevant to this discussion. It is unfortunate that at none of the sites have these early coins been found securely stratified in definitely pre-Roman contexts. Indeed many of them have no proper archaeological context at all.

All we can say with any degree of certainty therefore, is that there is evidence suggestive of a prehistoric presence at the later temple sites of Wanborough, Farley Heath and Titsey. The same is true at Chiddingfold and Ewell (see further below) and perhaps Frensham. At Betchworth and Westcott there are early enclosures and finds suggestive of ritual activity beginning in the early part of the first century AD but continuing after the 'invasion'. The

67 Conjectural reconstruction of the square temple at Wanborough. *Drawing: David Williams, courtesy Surrey Archaeological Society*

practice of making offerings in watery places (rivers, springs, marshes) also continued from prehistory into the Roman period and probably beyond; indeed it continues to be the case that people will throw coins into water in certain locations. Objects such as the bronze strainer of military type from near Thorpe and a nest of pewter plates found close to Shepperton in a silted-up river channel probably represent dedications of this kind.

The main changes introduced as a result of Britain becoming a Roman province were formal temples and new religions. The so-called Romano-Celtic temple is characteristic of the north-western provinces of the Empire and although not strictly a 'Roman' temple as such, it introduces the same idea, a formal home for the deity, that does not seem to have existed before. In plan the building is a square within a square, usually reconstructed as a central tower within an ambulatory (67). Other buildings can also sometimes be interpreted as temples. The new religions introduced in AD 43 included the official religions of the Roman state, to which all were expected to sacrifice on formal occasions, but these were not greatly different from the pre-existing religions, being also based in origin in the natural world. It was relatively easy to equate the attributes of local deities to those of the Roman gods, particularly Jupiter, Minerva, Mars and Mercury, with the result that on inscriptions they gained double names, such as the well-known Sulis Minerva at Bath, and Mars Camulos, now attested at Southwark *(85)*. This process is sometimes called *interpretatio romana*.

The Empire was wide-ranging and as a result Eastern mystery cults also came to be represented in Britain, including Christianity. The Empire was, of course, officially Christian for most of the fourth century, but the only certain evidence for Roman-period Christianity in Surrey is part of a jet ring found in excavations at Bagshot *(82)*. The ring has a rho-cross symbol on it, usually taken to be an early version of the better-known chi-rho (derived from the first letters of Christ's name in Greek). It has been claimed as evidence for a Roman Christian burial but the so-called grave is unconvincing and there is no evidence for a body. The site has not yet been published, but information already available suggests that it was unremarkable and at the moment little can be made of the presence of a Christian there, or how the ring came to be lost or discarded.

In general terms it might be anticipated that there were Christians in Southwark and perhaps some of the other larger settlements or the villas, but no evidence has been found as yet. Other eastern religions are represented mostly in these more Romanised environments, presumably reflecting the presence either of real outsiders or those most in contact with them. It is probable, however, that in Surrey, for most of the population most of the time, Romano-Celtic religion was the norm, including into the fourth century and perhaps beyond. Even in Southwark, although there is evidence for the eastern religions, the only known temples are Romano-Celtic in form and there are many ritual deposits in wells or shafts, a phenomenon also very noteworthy in Staines and Ewell.

Personal amulets with a religious significance were probably carried by most people, although only the most high status of people would have given their children a gold *bulla* like the one from Chelsham *(11)*. Others might carry leather pouches with materials thought to be lucky, or wear phallic pendants *(colour plate 3)*, which were regarded as a sign of good luck, and were often used by old people, women and children with the intention of warding off curses. Representations on rings might be regarded as protective by their owners, as for example one with the image of Mercury, found at Farley Heath *(colour plate 14)*. Such things as brooches could also have a meaning for the wearer, like the enamelled wheel brooches which could have been seen as a solar symbol *(colour plates 7, 14)*.

All households, in town and country, are likely to have had some sort of shrine although this would be difficult to prove. Where a tazza is found it may

68 'Lamp chimney' from Ashtead
Common (about 560mm high).
*Drawing: David Williams, from Bird
1987, fig 7.13*

indicate a household ritual involving the burning of incense. Several tazze were found at the Ashtead Common villa, which also produced fragments of a terra-cotta object that may have been a shrine, and pieces of the so-called 'lamp chimneys' *(68)* which probably also had some ritual purpose, for lamps and the burning of incense. There seem to be pieces of three or four different 'chimneys' from the Ashtead site, which is rather too many for a single household, but as their findspots are not clear it is possible that they were being manufactured there, perhaps to be supplied to other villas, or places like the Farley Heath temple, where one is reported.

In some cases separate shrines have been noted at villas, in circumstances where it is most likely that they were intended primarily for the use of those living at the site, like the apsidal-ended structure at Rapsley *(13, 37)*. The free-standing circular building at the Walton on the Hill villa has also been inter-preted as a shrine *(47)*, and two small free-standing buildings at Chiddingfold could have had a ritual purpose *(33)*. A small separate building between the two Titsey villas may be similar, but a more interesting possibility is that there was a shrine at the western end of the best-known building *(4)*. The very large

69 Bronze face mask from Titsey (about 60mm high). *Photograph: Brian Wood, courtesy Surrey Archaeological Society and Guildford Museum*

stone blocks there seem to be unnecessarily massive for a bath-house and one might speculate that they were part of an elaborate *nymphaeum*, to mark the spring that apparently rises here. The local place-name Pitchfont Lane, not far to the west, could suggest the presence of a special Roman *fontana* nearby (see chapter 11), and the bronze face mask was found not far away *(69)*. No doubt most villas had a built shrine of some sort, sometimes invisible to us within the main building complex. In some places, as suggested above, there may have been a temple-mausoleum, emphasising the importance of ancestors, or other indications of ritual activity, such as the filling of the well at Beddington. At the bottom, this had a horse's skull, leather shoes and pottery vessels, which will have been deliberate deposits associated with a ritual of termination of use.

Several finds suggest the influence of eastern religions at the villas: terracotta models of pine cones at Rapsley may be linked to worship of Attis, to be expected because of his link with Cybele, who is also probably represented there. Fragments of a large buff second-century pottery vessel with a mural crown and curls of hair, which ought to be linked to Cybele worship, were also found at the villa *(70, colour plate 10)*. A very fine bronze head of an ibis, presumably originally attached to some other material to represent the rest of the bird, is among the finds from Chiddingfold *(colour plate 3)*, and may be linked to an Egyptian religion. A Bes figurine from Abinger is also Egyptian, but as it is a chance find it is to be treated with caution as there is some evidence for the modern import of ancient finds to this site. A similar explanation has been offered for a finely decorated lamp from the Beddington area, which shows Attis, but it comes from an area known to include a number of Roman buildings and there is no particular reason to expect it to be a place in which a collector would lose a treasured find. Finally it should be noted that a small figurine supposedly of Aesculapius from Walton Heath has been reinterpreted as a river god – perhaps a curious choice for a site some distance from any river.

There were also special sacred sites in towns that provided for the needs of worshippers of the eastern religions. A very well-known find from Southwark is usually taken to indicate the presence of worshippers of Isis (an Egyptian deity): this is a complete flagon on which has been scratched *Londini ad fanum Isidis* ('in London at the shrine of Isis'). It may have come from the temple of Isis that is now attested on an inscription from the city proper, or even be a pot from an inn next door, but another shrine in Southwark would not be unexpected, given the plentiful evidence for overseas trade. A hunter god figure in a stone group recovered from below Southwark Cathedral has been linked to the worship of Attis with associated evidence suggesting that there may have been a shrine on the site.

Apart from this evidence suggesting eastern shrines, all the known temples in Surrey are Romano-Celtic; there is nothing to suggest classical-style buildings. Each of the towns and roadside settlements probably had some sort

70 Left Reconstruction of a mural-crowned head-pot. The five surviving examples are very fragmentary, and details, such as the facial features and the number of towers and gates on the wall, are conjectural. See also colour plate 10. Maximum diameter about 300mm. *Drawing: Joanna Bird*

71 Below Swan Street, Southwark: ritual burial. *Courtesy Pre-Construct Archaeology*

of sacred site regarded as housing the deity of the settlement. In some cases there may not have been a temple as such, but a place regarded as sacred where offerings might be made and ceremonials carried out. A possible site in Croydon has been suggested above, and it could also be true for the other settlements in Surrey except for Southwark, where temples are certainly known, although it seems more likely that places like Staines and Ewell will also have had proper temple structures.

Excavations within the last year or so by Pre-Construct Archaeology have revealed two small Romano-Celtic temples in Southwark, on the Tabard Square site. They were set in a sacred enclosure or *temenos*, which also included another building perhaps for the temple curators and features such as pits, in one of which the Mars Camulos inscription had been placed *(85)*. Reports on the objects from the site, including the *temenos* ditches, will be of great interest. The discovery of a sealed tin containing an ointment of some sort has already caused a stir. These temples were at a characteristic location, at the point where the roads arrived at the edge of the settlement *(18)*, and it is likely that there would have been another temple, or temples, inside. They were themselves near the cemeteries and there is other evidence for ritual activity in the immediate area, such as the 15 wells or shafts found in Swan Street. These dated to about AD 60-120; six had deliberately 'killed' pots in the fills and one contained the skeleton of an adult male head down, with a broken pot, four iron spikes and a dog skull *(71)*. Wells within the settlement proper also had ritual deposits, no doubt associated with termination; for instance one in Union Street had a triple vase set on a pottery ring and a fine set of antlers.

No certain ritual site has yet been located in Staines, but it might be noted that if there were buildings on the church 'island' they will have been in a similar position to those at Tabard Square in Southwark *(15, 18)*. Finds from the County Sports site near the Market Place are also suggestive. An early second-century round structure perhaps 5.5m across had a central pit with burnt material, too deep to be a hearth. An adjacent well or shaft had been backfilled in the early third century; at the bottom were several probably deliberately broken vessels, a complete quern and no less than 16 dogs. Other Staines wells or pits have produced finds of complete pots, suggestive of termination rituals; for example at the southern end of the Johnson & Clark site the remains of a well eroded by flooding contained four complete pots, part of a ring-base triple vase and part of a fine glass bowl.

The evidence from Ewell is similar, but there are some indications that the place as a whole may have had a religious character. The settlement is centred around the Hogsmill spring, which is of sufficient importance to have given the place its name: in Old English *aewiell*, meaning 'river spring'. Random digging near the spring has produced Roman-period finds that were probably votive offerings: coins, brooches and model weapons. Springs, with their

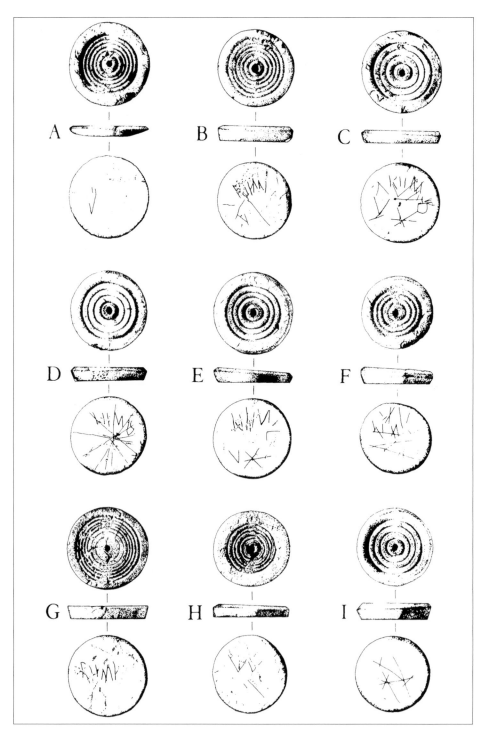

72 Bone counters from a burial at The Looe, near Ewell (about 22mm across). The marks V★ (on E for example) may mean '5 denarii', and RIIMI (REMI, clearest on G) could be short for *remittam*, 'I shall pay back'. Alternatively Remi may indicate '(property) of Remus'. *Drawing: Jonathan Cotton, from Bird 1987, fig 7.14*

obviously life-giving or life-sustaining aspect, were often venerated as sacred sites. Some were held to have healing properties, and since then as now health was a major concern, such springs could develop as places of pilgrimage, with provision for visitors. Those with some extra aspect might become of such importance that they gave rise to religious complexes or even large settlements. Bath is the prime British example, but a better parallel for Ewell might be Springhead (note the name) in Kent, where several temples have been found. At Springhead the Roman road goes through a double bend within the settlement in a similar fashion to that of the probable line of Stane Street at Ewell. There does not seem to be a topographical reason in either case, and it appears more likely that it was a deliberate way of drawing attention to the sacred focus of the site.

As well as the spring, Clive Orton has suggested that the King William IV site in Ewell *(23)* was a centre of ritual activity, probably from before the Roman period. Complete pots were found, and animal burials including at least two dogs, a horse and a deposit of horses' heads. A well or shaft on the site had been backfilled with layered deposits that included cattle bones, pottery, jewellery and coins. On the southern edge of the settlement at Purberry Shot another well, about 40ft (12m) deep, was apparently backfilled when a road was built over it. The published report is not very helpful but it is probable that it also had layered deposits; there was a great deal of pottery in the fill but the upper ten feet (3m) had a few almost complete pots, and the contents also included two brooches, a glass bead, components of four manicure sets, a possibly pre-Roman razor, an 'ox-goad' and a knife. Not far away at the site known as The Looe storage pits had been backfilled with special deposits including largely complete cattle and dogs, a human cremation burial with associated gaming counters *(72)*, noted above, and a nearby sheep or goat cremation placed in a complete pot.

The examples of filled pits or shafts so far discussed may all have originally been dug for a different purpose, as a well or a storage pit, but on the south-eastern outskirts of Ewell there were several shafts that must have been dug for no other purpose than ritual. They are too deep for pits and in the wrong place to be wells, although they are not far from the settlement, being 400m south of the King William IV site and only 150m from the nearest part of the building straggle, on rising ground near and east of Stane Street *(23)*. At least ten shafts were recognised in a chalk quarry in the mid nineteenth century *(24)*. Hugh Diamond was able to record the fills of six of them, which were between 12 and 37ft (3.6 and 11.7m) deep and 2ft 2 in to 4ft (66–122cm) in diameter. He noted that there were different layers in the fill, from the top: large animal bones – cattle, sheep, stag and pig; then samian vessels, some complete, but several mended with lead; then a 'fine rich mould' with shells of oyster, mussel and snail; then fragments of amphorae; and finally, dark coloured vessels, several complete, with charcoal and other signs of burning – apparently including burnt human bone and unburnt animal bone. Diamond says that the arrangement he describes was repeated three times over in two of the deepest pits. Taking the shafts as a whole, the 'fine rich mould' layer also included apple pips, cherry stones, a small bronze ring, brooches, unidentified bits of bronze, glass fragments including square bottles, and bones of cock, hare and dog, in one case a complete large dog but with the head placed about a foot from the body. Other finds of interest included iron objects, possibly related to the priestly regalia known from other Surrey sites. The fills of two other shafts were recorded later in the nineteenth century and found to be similar; again there was a great deal of pottery, iron objects and indications of decayed bronzes and animal bones including ox, 'boar', hare, fowl, and a stag's antlers.

The different and repeated layers clearly indicate ritual activity over a period of time. The evidence suggests that there may have been different ceremonies at different times of year or perhaps phases over a lengthy ritual process. All the elements known from other ritual shafts are found: whole pots, some deliberately smashed; bones of significant animals, some complete – but sometimes oddly placed, for example with the head separated; even human bones (as in the Southwark well: *71*). Some Romano-British shafts are known to have been associated with temples, and it is possible that this was the case in Ewell. Jonathan Cotton is pursuing reports of the recent discoveries on a site nearby which apparently included a well or shaft and a possible building, with several associated complete potttery vessels, mostly of samian ware.

TEN

COUNTRYSIDE AND
CEREMONY

The special religious needs of the bulk of the rural population were served by going to important sacred sites in town or countryside. The latter perhaps had a special sanctity going back into prehistory. Current evidence suggests that not all of these sites came to have temples as such and this aspect is discussed later. We know of four certain temple buildings in the Surrey countryside: two at Wanborough and one each at Farley Heath and Titsey. Each place had one of the standard Romano-Celtic temples and Wanborough also had another temple that was more or less circular in plan. The first two sites are comparatively well-known from excavation but that at Titsey has had less attention. Each of these sites is a scheduled monument, but this legal protection has not prevented the activities of unprincipled looters.

The site at Wanborough first came to attention as a scatter of Roman pottery in the 1960s, and subsequent fieldwork indicated the presence of buildings. In 1983 two metal detectorists found 12 gold and silver coins (mostly Iron Age), which they reported. Unfortunately the findspot became known to treasure hunters who began to loot the site in increasing numbers. As the scale of the damage increased it became necessary to mount a rescue excavation, which was arranged by Surrey Archaeological Society following a major fund-raising campaign. The excavation showed that an area of more than 200 sq metres had been destroyed just to the west of a Romano-Celtic temple, whose plan survived as foundations or robber trenches (73). Where stratigraphy survived, under the temple or along the hedgerow (where it had not been undermined by the looters), there were traces of a dark layer pre-dating the temple which had probably contained most of the thousands of coins known to have come from

73 The Wanborough temple under excavation in 1985, with damage caused by treasure hunters in the background. *Photograph: author*

the site as well as bronze priestly regalia, pottery and burnt bone. The temple was the usual square within a square in plan, the inner one having deeper foundations which gives support to the usual interpretation as a tower *(67)*. This inner room (the *cella*) was probably built of flint with greensand levelling courses and quoins and a tiled roof; it was a little over 6m square inside and was probably paved with an ironstone tessellated floor, perhaps with a red and white border or patterning. The walls were plastered and painted dull red and a creamy white, with some indications of other colours. The ambulatory around the *cella* was floored with large slabs of greensand.

The site was backfilled and covered with a greater depth of soil in an effort to prevent treasure hunting, but this continued, albeit at a reduced level. Geophysical survey was carried out in the field by English Heritage in 1997 which suggested a number of features including a semi-circular feature to the south of the known temple. In 1999 further excavation was carried out to test these features and then extended to rescue the plan of a building considered to be under threat *(74)*. This building has been interpreted as a circular temple *(75)*, while the semi-circular feature was found to be a metalled trackway. At its western end there appeared to be another surfaced area adjacent to a water hole (labelled 'shaft' on the plan). There were indications of more metalling around the circular temple.

There are a few hints that the site may have been of significance in the pre-Roman period: pieces of probable prehistoric pottery and a few metal objects (although the latter could be Roman-period offerings). The 'water hole' may be pre-Roman. It is generally accepted, however, that the thousands of Iron Age gold and silver coins, many of them Atrebatic, were deposited as a hoard not long after the conquest in a group that included several Roman Republican and some early Imperial silver pieces. There may have been some sort of shrine structure at this time but the first certain temple was the circular building, perhaps constructed at about the end of the first century AD. Around the middle of the second century it seems to have suffered a catastrophic

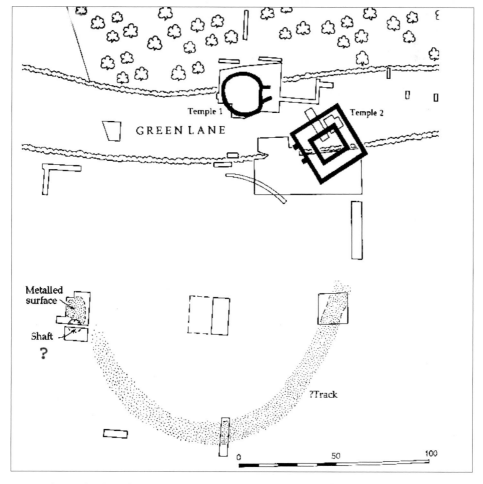

74 Wanborough: plan of the site showing the main features known from excavation and geophysical survey. *Drawing: David Williams*

75 Wanborough: the circular temple under excavation, looking west across the entrance.
Photograph: David Williams

collapse and it is likely that it was then replaced by the square temple. As part
of a dedicatory process it seems that offerings represented by pottery and burnt
bone were first spread on the site together with the priestly regalia associated
with the circular temple and very large numbers of coins. This theory has the
advantage of explaining the survival of the regalia and such large numbers of
good quality coins on the site (far more than anywhere else in Britain). If the
collapse of the first temple was, as it were, an act of god, then the desire for a
splendid dedicatory process for the new building would be very understand-
able. The square temple may have lasted into the later fourth century before it
was demolished; coins show activity at the site to the very end of the Roman
period. The available evidence hints that there were also nearby buildings
which presumably acted as housing for temple curators and visitors. The water
hole may have been a key ritual feature approached by the semi-circular track
but the shape of the latter as indicated by geophysical survey undoubtedly calls
to mind a small theatre, which would not be out of place on a religious site. It
may be that the track curved round a box-framed structure providing several
tiers of seats in a semi-circle, which would have left very little evidence that
could be traced archaeologically.

A temple on Farley Heath was first mentioned by Aubrey in the early eighteenth century and Martin Tupper excavated extensively there in the 1840s (part
of his poem about this work is given in the introductory chapter). The site also

received attention from Winbolt in 1927, and later on Lowther and Goodchild together. Only the two last-named produced a report worthy of the name, and Goodchild was also able to track down some of the more significant of Tupper's finds, and offer fresh interpretation of the site and the unique sceptre binding *(81)*. Tupper's saving grace was that he commissioned a very fine set of coloured drawings of some of the best finds from Benjamin Nightingale *(colour plate 14)*; Winbolt's finds drawings, by contrast, are so bad that it is difficult to match them to the actual objects supposedly from his excavations now held in Guildford Museum. As with many Roman religious sites in Britain, Farley Heath has had its share of attacks from treasure hunters, even though it is a site protected by law, and recently it was decided that what was left should be salvaged by one final excavation, carried out by the Surrey County Archaeological Unit with funding from English Heritage. This was able to confirm details of the temple and its surrounding enclosure, and its publication will be accompanied by a full illustrated catalogue of all the finds known to have come from the site, making it possible to appreciate in full their quality and quantity.

Farley Heath had a Romano-Celtic temple similar in shape and size to the one at Wanborough. It was constructed mostly from the local greensand, including the harder Bargate stone, and had a tiled roof. Small fragments of surviving wall plaster indicate that it was painted red and white as at Wanborough, with several other colours to make patterns. Flooring did not survive in situ but floor tiles and tesserae made from tile and from ironstone were found. Perhaps the ambulatory was floored with tiles and the *cella* was tessellated. The temple was set within a walled *temenos*, although very much off centre *(colour plate 13)*. An irregular polygonal area was enclosed, apparently unique in Britain. The two lines of walling on the northern side suggest different phases, but it is not known which is the earlier. Many finds of coins, metal objects, pottery and animal bones were made within the *temenos*, mostly by Tupper, and they suggest that the site was in use from before the Roman period to the beginning of the fifth century or beyond. Winbolt apparently also found a pit full of iron. No other buildings are known, but outside the defined ritual area one or two possible pottery kilns and ovens have been found and it has been claimed that a nearby pond has Roman-period paving.

The Titsey temple was first excavated in 1879 by Leveson-Gower, although he did not recognise it as such. It was re-examined in 1935 by James Graham, who identified the temple and extended operations to the *temenos* wall and the course of the Roman road adjacent to the site, although he does not seem to have done much work within the *temenos*. The temple *cella* was nearly square, with internal dimensions of about 15ft (4.6m); it was surrounded by traces of an ambulatory defined mostly by debris from the medieval robbing of the site. The *cella* had deep flint foundations and probably had a tiled roof. It was set on the eastern side of a *temenos* about 100ft (31m) square, defined by a flint wall (with occasional pieces of sandstone). Outside the south-eastern corner an area of burnt material and sandstone slabs was thought to mark the site of an oven, although it could have been medieval. In view of the lack of excavation in the *temenos* and the extensive disturbance in the medieval period, no meaningful assessment can be made of the quality or quantity of finds, about which little is known. Graham notes the presence of fossil sea urchins but assumes that they were brought in with loads of gravel. They have, however, been found at both the other temple sites and are likely to have been offerings.

The temple is sited alongside the Roman road from London to the Lewes area, very close to a spring which is a source of the River Eden, and close to another feeding into the Darenth *(76)*. It is possible therefore that part of the religious power of the place derived from this fact. Water was needed at religious sites for various purposes including ritual cleansing, so the presence of a spring, well or pond should not on its own be taken to imply that this was part of the special meaning of the site, but important springs often gave rise to sacred sites in the ancient world and this may have been the main reason for the siting of the Titsey temple. If it was associated with the nearby villa then this might explain its location over 1.5km distant. The temple is supposed to have been short-lived, but in view of the limited excavation and medieval robbing any dating should be treated with caution, although it is noteworthy that Iron Age pottery is reported from the site. It is possible the complex was of greater importance than is currently recognised: finds from the excavations included box flue-tiles, with one fragment coming from well outside the *temenos*, near the spring. This would be a suitable location for a bath-house and other buildings to house visitors.

Another possible spring-related religious complex may have existed near Chiddingfold, deep in the Weald in the south-west of the county. The site has been interpreted as a villa, but as such would be easily Surrey's largest, although apparently in the least favourable situation, surrounded by the Weald Clay. It is a large complex of buildings which suggests considerable resources and in such cases we would normally expect formal planning around a courtyard or central space and some indication of one or more high quality mosaic floors. At Chiddingfold there are indications of tessellated floors but only of the most basic sort. The complex gives the impression of being an accumulation of additional buildings with no overall planning. This is difficult to parallel at villas elsewhere, but unplanned grouping of buildings can be found at religious sites, such as at Nettleton (Wiltshire) and Uley (Gloucestershire). They usually include one or more temples and other buildings providing rooms to cater for the needs of visitors.

Other aspects of the site might support a religious interpretation. It is set on high ground with very extensive views in all directions. Such prominent siting is very characteristic of Roman religious sites in the countryside. The isolated setting, probably surrounded by dense woodland, would also be appropriate. The buildings seem to have been enclosed within a polygonal wall, which is most unusual but could find a parallel in the *temenos* wall at Farley Heath. Two

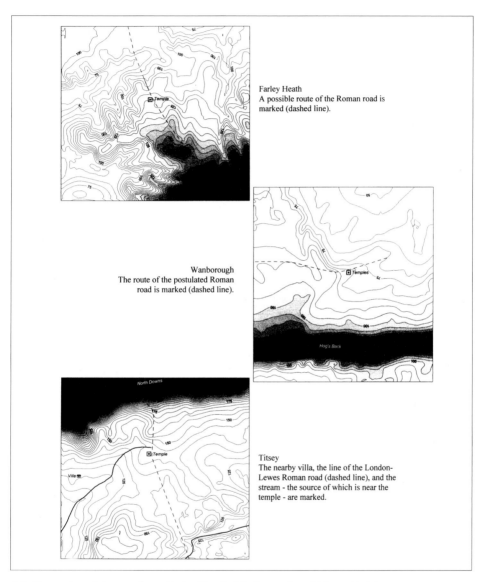

Farley Heath
A possible route of the Roman road is
marked (dashed line).

Wanborough
The route of the postulated Roman
road is marked (dashed line).

Titsey
The nearby villa, the line of the London-
Lewes Roman road (dashed line), and the
stream - the source of which is near the
temple - are marked.

76 The setting of the temples at Farley Heath, Wanborough and Titsey. Heights in metres.
Drawing: David and Audrey Graham

small square structures standing apart from the other buildings may have been separate shrines, but the results of a recent detailed fieldwalking survey suggest that the main shrine might have been east of the known buildings and nearer the spring. Finds of ceramic building material and tesserae were plotted and seen to coincide with the known plan except for a noted concentration not associated with any known building *(33)*.

The site is near the headwaters of the Arun, and has a good spring very near the top of the hill (which is itself a sandy soil but immediately over clay). This phenomenon may have been regarded as unusual, leading to the development of some sort of spring-related cult which could provide the explanation for the strange circular stone-built 'tanks' noted at various parts of the site in the nineteenth-century excavations. The best preserved of these was said to be '3 feet 6 inches [1m] deep with a stone foundation [presumably base]; the sides were also stoned to the full depth in regular courses, and the opening was 2 feet [60cm] square'. It is not possible to be sure that these features were Roman in date (although it would be difficult to explain their presence at any other period), but a circular shallow basin in one room is specifically described as being set at Roman floor level and T.S. Cooper, the excavator, was obviously convinced that it was contemporary.

The finds from Chiddingfold that have survived are not especially supportive of a religious function for the site; most of the material is the normal range of pottery, although its widespread origins are perhaps noteworthy. There are a few finds likely to be of ritual significance in their own right, particularly the bronze ibis head *(colour plate 3)*, a small face mask, perhaps related to the Titsey example and connected with a cult of the head, two Venus figurines and a pottery mural crown *(70, colour plate 10)*, but these are probably no more than would be expected at a normal villa. It is likely, however, that many finds were dispersed before they reached a museum. In particular Cooper noted a 'huge rubbish heap', which he described as containing 'a very large quantity of pottery of nearly every description found, as well as bronze objects, coins and some flint arrowheads'. This is a strange rubbish heap; it would not be unreasonable to conclude that it might instead be a large spread of votive offerings. The arrowheads are particularly interesting in this respect, as they must have been collected deliberately, if they were really part of the same deposit, and their use as votive offerings would be the best explanation in a Roman context.

It is possible therefore to reinterpret Chiddingfold as a religious site, set at a prominent location deep in the Weald at an important water source (one perhaps regarded as having healing properties). The complex would then be seen as having one or more free-standing shrines within a defined sacred area and buildings providing for the needs of pilgrims.

We cannot be sure that Chiddingfold was a religious centre, but there are other sites where although a ritual interpretation seems certain, no evidence can be found for associated temples or built shrines of any kind. In fact there is clear evidence from some temple sites in Britain and abroad that the temple can be secondary to some more important feature, such as a sacred tree. Probably all sacred sites in the countryside began in this way, and some, perhaps many, did not come to have temples. Obviously this can make them difficult to recognise, but groups of finds can provide significant evidence. For example, material recovered from a former stream crossing in Kingston included 355 coins, some apparently ritually 'killed' and probably deposited across the period around AD 320-60, together with broken jewellery. A site near Frensham has produced several hundred coins, part of a special bronze vessel, fragments of the iron binding of a sceptre handle *(77)* and 65 miniature pots *(78)*, two of which are thought to have held cannabis. A hillside nearby would be a suitable place for a temple but testing has proved negative so far. Near Westcott excavation of a section across the ditch of an enclosure known from aerial photography has produced many finds suggestive of ritual continuing from the Iron Age into the early Roman period.

Further east at Betchworth another enclosure *(10)*, probably of similar date, is likely to have been continuing a ritual tradition starting at least as far back as the Neolithic period (suggested by large amounts of Grooved Ware pottery). The enclosure is too small for a house but included a pit with a burnt deposit with two animal jaws; the western ditch contained a large amount of pottery and some cremated animal bone. Cut into the outer edge of this ditch were five ovens and a sixth was set high in the ditch fill. Part of a pottery vessel was found near this site many years ago, probably in a sandpit perhaps 500-600m away; it had a specially-made applied figure representing the native Jupiter *(79)*. Finally, a site near Godstone may be mentioned where carefully recorded metal detecting has produced several hundred coins and many brooches with some other metal objects. Recent geophysical survey has revealed that the finds may be associated with the ditches of one or more enclosures, and a ritual explanation is among the possible interpretations.

It is not clear why some sacred sites 'grew' temples while others did not, but it must be likely that a major part was played by people who held important roles within the *civitas*. It is evident that the temples use the same building techniques as villas, and this must indicate the involvement of those who would think in terms of building like this and be able to find the resources and expertise. In fact the elite would have been expected to play a major role in the construction and upkeep of the temples, either directly or acting on behalf of the governing council. It is possible also that major temples in the countryside had a semi-official function, providing the opportunity at the special ceremonies to promulgate *civitas* or provincial messages to the wider populace. This may be another reason why major rural temples are often found filling the gaps between towns. They may also relate in some way to subdivisions of a *civitas*.

In general, Romano-British temples or sacred sites are found at characteristic locations in the countryside, in particular on or near hill tops or locally

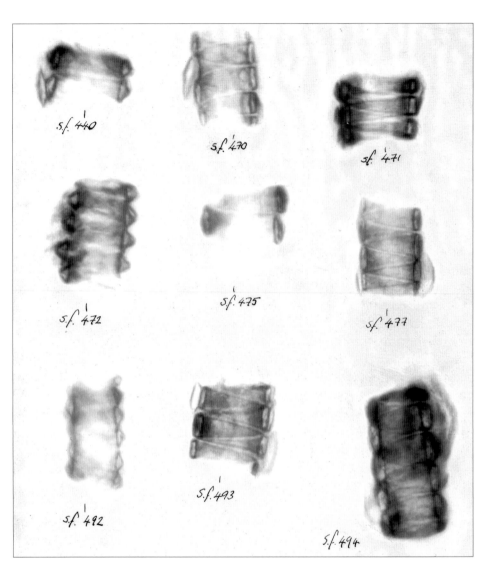

s.f. 440

s.f. 470

s.f. 471

s.f. 472

s.f. 475

s.f. 477

s.f. 492

s.f. 493

s.f. 494

77 Frensham: x-ray photographs of fragments of iron sceptre bindings. *Courtesy Museum of Farnham*

78 Frensham: miniature pots from the ritual site. *Photograph: David Graham*

important high ground. It is noteworthy that all of the Surrey temples could
have been set at higher positions if that had been required *(76)*; in particular
Wanborough is very near to the Hog's Back ridge and Titsey is only just south
of the North Downs scarp. It may be that part of the point was that they could
be seen from the higher ground, standing out from their surroundings. They
will have had prominent towers with red tiled roofs and may have been
plastered and painted white or red outside. Interestingly, most of the other
ritual sites mentioned are also on rising ground visible from the Downs, and
this throws into prominence some other Surrey religious sites, for the medieval
churches or chapels at Wotton, St Martha's Hill, and St Catherine's Hill are in
very similar locations. There is, however, no good evidence to indicate that
they are successors to earlier ritual sites, although the curiousity of their siting
is often remarked.

Where this can be tested Romano-Celtic temples prove to have east-facing
entrances, which should be kept in mind when considering if there was a formal
approach to any particular site. Other common characteristics in Britain include
siting at or near earlier monuments such as hill forts or barrows, at springs, in
association with special trees or groves, by roads or on significant boundaries.
Many temples are at sites that fit more than one of these categories and this is
the case with Surrey's known temples. Titsey, for example, is on a road, near a
spring, set on a locally important high spot and possibly at a boundary (if the

79 Left Betchworth: appliqué on fragment of pottery vessel showing a native Jupiter-type god. *Photograph: Brian Wood, courtesy Surrey Archaeological Society and Guildford Museum*

Surrey–Kent border marks an earlier division of some sort). The relationship of this temple with the London–Lewes road is of considerable interest *(76)*. It is situated at a point where the road changed direction; the effect would have been as though the long straight stretch from the south was heading directly at the temple. This is one of a number of examples where the siting of temples has affected or been affected by the course of a Roman road: possible cases in Ewell and Southwark have already been noted.

Wanborough may be a relatively rare example of a temple in a sacred grove; the temples are sited on London Clay and even today the area is heavily wooded *(29)*. The bounds of a sacred clearing perhaps defined the *temenos* as no evidence for a constructed boundary has yet been noted. The isolation of the site may be more apparent than real, however, as there is increasing evidence for Roman-period settlement in the area north of the Hog's Back and there may have been a major road (from London to Winchester) close by. Farley Heath is alongside a road, on high ground, although again it is noteworthy that it is not at the highest point *(76)*. It seems to have been set to be visible from north, east and west and may have been seen as marking the boundary with the Weald beyond. Visibility would depend on the area being heathland, and there is some evidence that this was the case in the Roman period. Wanborough may also have been seen as at a boundary with the 'wild', in this case to the north, and this aspect needs further consideration generally;

a much lower population would have meant that large parts of the county will have felt quite empty and in the hands of 'nature'. Even in the 1980s and close to Guildford, the Wanborough site felt quite isolated.

Evidence for the use of these sacred sites is mostly confined to the temples, and the following extract from one of Pliny the Younger's letters gives some idea of what might have been involved:

> I am told by the soothsayers that I must rebuild the temple of Ceres which stands on my property; it needs enlarging and improving, for it is certainly very old and too small considering how crowded it is on its special anniversary, when great crowds gather there from the whole district on 13 September and many ceremonies are performed and vows made and discharged. But there is no shelter nearby from rain or sun, so I think it will be an act of generosity and piety alike to build as fine a temple as I can and add porticoes – the temple for the goddess and the porticoes for the public ... we shall also have to have made a statue of the goddess, for several pieces are broken off the original wooden one as it is so old. (Radice 1963, 258-9)

Although this refers to Italy, available evidence suggests that it can be readily paralleled in this country. For instance, the system of making and paying vows is known throughout the Empire and is well attested in Britain by lead tablets from places like Bath and Uley, and by inscriptions on stone altars. Evidence is mostly lacking in Surrey, no doubt because the county is far from the usual sources of lead and has no stone suitable for inscriptions. There is a possible lead vow from Farley Heath but it must be likely that it was normal in this area to use organic materials that have not survived. There is some support for this idea from finds made at Wanborough. Two seal-box lids found there would have been intended to contain the wax seals of documents (usually the formal writing tablets); it is reasonable to assume that they would have been sealing written vows or requests to the deity. Finds of seal-box lids are rare in Surrey, so it is interesting that two more examples are known from possibly sacred sites in Ewell (the King William IV site and the Hogsmill spring area). There were also two iron items usually interpreted as ox-goads at Wanborough, but recent finds at Vindolanda have suggested that these might be better interpreted as pen nibs. The use of thin strips of wood for written vows, like the letters found at Vindolanda, would make good sense in Surrey. Our sites may also have had well-made inscriptions on wood; they were used even in formal military contexts as rare finds show. Only exceptional circumstances would preserve them, as would be the case with wooden statues of deities, again to be expected in this area of poor quality stone. Such things existed even in Italy, as Pliny's letter shows.

An image of the deity of the place would be expected inside the temple *cella*, which was not intended for use by worshippers. Instead, ceremonies were held, and offerings made, outside. The making and payment of vows was obviously a private matter for each individual, and if matters were pressing presumably a special trip to the temple might be made on such an occasion. Where we have written evidence in Britain (not, unfortunately in Surrey), the deity might be asked for help with a wide variety of problems: different aspects of health, the return of stolen goods, assistance with a love affair, a journey or a business deal and so on. If the god delivered, then payment of the vow was required and might involve offerings which must have been relevant in the minds of the dedicators, at least. Pottery and glass vessels presumably indicate food and drink that we cannot now trace, except where meat on the bone was offered; complete animals seem to be more common in ritual shaft ceremonies. Personal items were frequent offerings at Surrey temples: brooches *(colour plate 14)*, earrings, necklaces, bracelets, hairpins, belt fittings, shoes (represented now by hobnails) and presumably other items of clothing (sometimes mentioned in written vows), toilet articles such as nail cleaners, fittings that represent boxes, a variety of metalwork, perhaps associated with someone's trade, or weapons appropriate to a deity's martial aspect (these might include antiques, such as Neolithic or Bronze Age axes). Coins were sometimes offered; there is some evidence to suggest that the good quality ones were regarded as contributions to the upkeep of the shrine and periodically gathered in for that purpose. Even special stones were dedicated: pebbles from distant locations have been noted at Wanborough, one of the Ewell shafts had a collection of several round flint stones, and there were fossils at all three Surrey temple sites.

As Pliny's letter suggests, the temples also had an important community role, providing occasions for regular gatherings. There is some evidence for annual or more frequent ceremonies, no doubt in origin linked to important times in the agricultural year. Animal bones recovered at British temple sites suggest sacrifices at certain times of year, and it is reasonable to assume that these occasions were rather like medieval fairs. We can imagine processions, ceremonials and feasting, all with a religious component but providing also much-needed entertainment. Ovens or related structures are known at the King William IV site in Ewell, near the County Sports site in Staines, at Farley Heath, Betchworth and possibly Titsey. Hearths have been noted near Wanborough too. Ceremonials need a stage, and the possibility of a theatre-type structure at Wanborough has been highlighted above.

At the main temple sites, whether in town or country, the officiating priest will have been a member of the elite of the *civitas*, as attested in Gaul and Germany. We know something of the ceremonial dress of Surrey's priests from finds at Wanborough, Farley Heath and elsewhere. The Wanborough regalia include several unique chain headdresses, most with attached wheels, and a large number of bronze sceptre handles, some with associated binding for the shafts *(colour plates 11, 12)*. The headdresses were made of four bronze chains attached to a central disc and then connected to each other by another chain

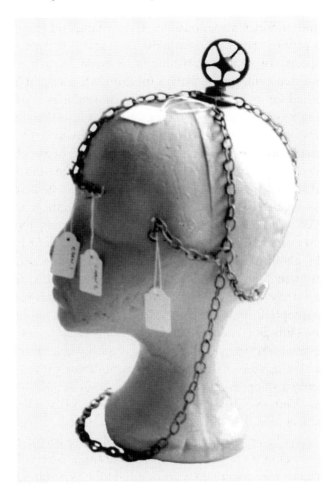

80 The best-surviving
Wanborough headdress,
mounted on a dummy head.
The different lengths of the
chains at the front and back
of the head show clearly.
Photograph: author

circling the brow, with a further chain hanging down from near the ear
positions, forming a sort of necklace *(80)*. One at least of the Wanborough
examples had a fine leaf pendant on this necklace. The headdress was probably
mounted on a leather cap, which may itself have had attached antlers, to judge
from the representation on a unique Iron Age coin from near Petersfield. The
silver plaque representing an ear of corn may also have been attached to a
headdress *(colour plate 3)*.

A chain headdress *(colour plate 12)* and a spike finial probably from another
one are known from Farley Heath, which also has a unique decorated bronze
sceptre binding *(81)*. When found, this was still in a spiral shape from wrapping
round the wooden shaft, and it had an iron finial for the end of the shaft. Two
small bronze bird figurines from the temple site, an eagle and an owl, may have
served as sceptre ends. Fragments of the iron binding for a sceptre are known
from Frensham *(77)* and an iron object mentioned in Diamond's report on the

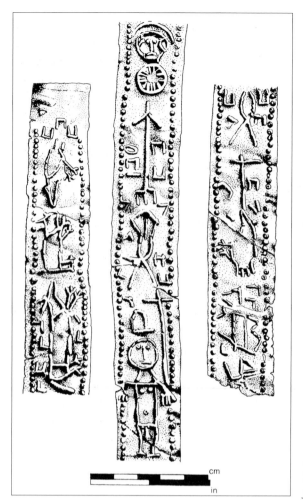

81 The Farley Heath sceptre
binding. *Drawing: David Williams,
from Bird 1987, fig 7.16*

Ewell shafts also sounds as though it could be a sceptre: 'an iron rod, 2ft8in
(810mm) in length, ornamented at each end', although what could be this
object in the British Museum has been identified as a tripod leg. Bronze
objects that could have had special qualities as heirlooms may have been used
for the pouring of libations at Frensham (a fine jug known as an *askos*) and
Farley Heath (a ladle with a duck's head handle, a *cyathus*, which would have
been something of an antiquity by the mid-first century) *(colour plate 14)*.
Beautiful enamelled miniature 'stools' from the latter site will also have had
some ritual use. They were designed as sets of threes, diminishing in size to sit
on top of one another; the surface area of the two Farley Heath examples
indicates that two sets are involved.

Unfortunately, because of the lack of inscriptions, we have no direct
evidence for the names of the local deities of Surrey, although we can identify

some of their aspects from the evidence of the priestly regalia and the offerings. The wheel motif at Wanborough is associated with the Celtic solar god, equated with Jupiter, and the spirally bound sceptres probably represent his lightning bolts. The Celtic Jupiter figure on the Betchworth pot *(79)* carries lightning and a staff. The wheel god appears again at Farley Heath, on the sceptre binding, which also has the smith-god, marked by his hammer and tongs, and perhaps by his dog and even stag. His Gaulish equivalent is usually called Succellos, and the raven on the binding is thought to be representative of his consort, Nantosuelta, but all three animals are also linked with death. An East Gaulish samian pot at Farley Heath was probably carefully chosen because it was decorated with dogs and stags and there is a similar earlier samian vessel from one of the Ewell shafts. Perhaps the decoration on the die 6 tiles from Ashtead *(58, colour plate 8)* had some extra purpose. As we have seen, complete dogs are a common find in ritual shafts and backfilled wells and pits; antlers are also found.

The evidence suggests that local deities may have had a mixture of attributes so that we can talk of a sun-god/Celtic Jupiter aspect such as the wheel but note also other elements suggestive of a smith-god or finds indicating a Mercury-type deity or yet others, all from the same site, as in the case of Farley Heath. It is best to assume that the deity was first and foremost local to the site or perhaps the tribal group, and could take on several different aspects depending on the needs of the worshipper. An equation with any particular Roman god is probably to be treated with a degree of caution, as the deity needed to be able to help with the wide variety of problems people have. Specialisation was perhaps only a matter for the famous healing shrines. Other places could probably take dedications to any vaguely relevant god, an aspect well-illustrated by the Mars Camulos inscription *(85)*. Although found at a temple site in Southwark, this was dedicated by a member of the Bellovaci, from the area around Beauvais in northern France, to the god local to that region.

There are some signs that there were elements common to the Surrey area: chain headdresses (uncommon in the rest of Britain) from Farley Heath and Wanborough; wheel symbols at both sites; spiral sceptre bindings at both and at Frensham (and the Celtic Jupiter pot from Betchworth); fossil sea urchins at both and at Titsey; dogs and stags widely represented. This last is of interest in contrast to Sussex, where there is evidence for boar cults apparently not seen in Surrey. Another contrast is the lack of evidence from Surrey for any religious sites associated with earlier monuments such as hillforts and barrows. A Surrey – Sussex (Atrebatic?) link is, however, suggested by the Cybele pots *(70)*, as similar vessels are known from Rapsley, Chiddingfold, Alfoldean, Fishbourne and Beddingham, the last three in Sussex, and they were probably made in that county at the Wiggonholt potteries. It may be relevant in this context to note that both Rapsley and Beddingham have produced evidence for free-standing apsidal-ended buildings interpreted as shrines.

Wanborough, Farley Heath and some of the other probable ritual sites have coin evidence indicating continuity of use up to the end of the Roman period. The temples as such may have been in a state of collapse but this could be partly because of the withdrawal of elite support; at least some of the villas were being abandoned and of course it would have been sensible to be at least not visibly non-Christian. Temple structures were, however, not an important part of the sanctity of a site, as already argued. We do not know when the sites went out of use, but it is interesting to speculate that some of them might have continued into the Saxon period. If it is right to assume that parts of the county remained in 'British' hands for some time after the coming of the Saxons, and that they were eventually assimilated, then it is logical to assume that some of the countryside shrines continued in use. It may even be that the places recorded in Saxon place-names as pagan shrines were Romano-British in origin, which might hint at Roman-period sacred sites at such places as Thunderfield, near Horley. It would not have been difficult to equate our lightning-wielding god with Thunor.

ELEVEN

THE END OF
ROMAN SURREY

We are not yet able to say much about the history of Roman Surrey, the way things changed through time, but it is clear enough that the later period differed considerably from the earlier one, hardly surprising in a span of nearly 400 years. In general the first two centuries were more what most people think of as 'Roman' and the last two much less so. There are signs of landscape change from about AD 200, and this may be linked to the literary evidence for the rise of larger land-holdings and peasants increasingly tied to the land (and perhaps explains signs of decline at some sites). Surrey's villas were at their most developed later on, some apparently even starting late, although there is little to suggest that a few grew larger at the expense of others, as happened elsewhere in Britain. Coin finds imply some sort of occupation at most villas until the end of the Roman period, but in general the evidence is too limited to indicate what state they were in. The later period is marked by large native pottery industries like Alice Holt/Farnham, and poor quality coinage. The presence of the latter, however, presumably indicates continuing commercial activity in towns, especially as it was not worth the metal it was made from. Town life, as in the countryside, was probably more 'medieval'. There were also changes in burial practices, and in the kinds of offerings at temples. Christianity became the official religion *(82)*, but the rural pagan temples continued in use.

Literary evidence shows that the later Empire was under great pressure from barbarians and that there were often internal power struggles, in some of which British forces became involved. The Roman army itself became increasingly

169

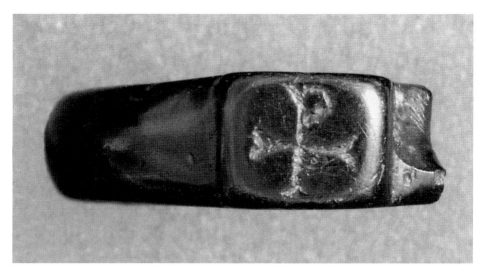

82 Jet ring from Bagshot with rho-cross symbol. *Photograph: David Stokes, courtesy Surrey Heath Archaeological and Heritage Trust*

Germanised, in the end often using barbarian tribal units. Some of the known events probably affected our area, in particular London/Southwark, but this would have had a knock-on effect, especially along the roads out from the capital. In AD 296 the short-lived British-based empire of Carausius and Allectus was brought to a close by imperial forces. The main body of troops under Asclepiodotus landed in the Solent and headed for London, so perhaps for the second time a Roman military commander crossed Surrey at the head of an invading force. Increasing barbarian attacks probably had little effect locally, but in AD 367 a so-called *barbarica conspiratio* saw many different groups get together to overrun the province, and order was not restored until AD 369. None of this has been recognised in the Surrey archaeological record. The end of Rapsley looks dramatic, with two buildings set on fire, but the date (about AD 330) and other evidence suggests that the site was carefully abandoned.

The archaeological record for the fourth and fifth centuries is, however, very inadequate, which is unfortunate as it is clear that Surrey is a key area for understanding the transition from Roman Britain to Saxon England. One problem is the dating evidence, for there are no imports of official coinage after AD 402, and the huge pottery industries come to an end. Another problem is that late levels on Roman sites are the most likely to be disturbed by later activity; where they do survive they have rarely been excavated using adequate techniques. It is abundantly clear from work elsewhere that meticulous area excavations with careful planning of what seems to be no more than fallen rubble can reveal evidence of continued activity on what was thought to be an abandoned site. There are a few hints suggesting continuity into the fifth century, such as a strap terminal from the Chelsham villa and some of the finds from the Saxon cemeteries. The real problem is closing the gap between the early fifth and later fifth century, a matter of perhaps two generations. Continuity is probably impossible to prove archaeologically: for example, a villa may be abandoned but its estate could continue to be worked from a new dwelling site, using the same boundaries. Do Saxon burials near a Roman site mean continued use of that site or just coincidence? It may be noted that where Roman roads continue in existence this is likely to indicate that they did not go out of use.

There is an important group of early Saxon cemeteries in north-east Surrey at Croydon, Beddington and Mitcham *(83)*. They probably began in the later fifth century and certainly continued in use into the sixth or seventh, but there are hints that they were sited next to existing burial grounds. For instance a Roman-type burial on the edge of the Croydon cemetery has been dated by radiocarbon methods to the early fifth century, and there are early records of stone coffins with the Mitcham Saxon burials. These cemeteries form part of a ring round London from Mucking in Essex to Shepperton, and it is reasonable to suppose that they represent groups originally placed to guard the

83 Mitcham Saxon cemetery, grave 73, probably later sixth century. Sword on left side, knife to left of waist, spear on right side (head above right shoulder), shield over legs (boss on right shin bone), iron boar's head buckle from clothing. *From Bidder and Morris 1959, plate 23*

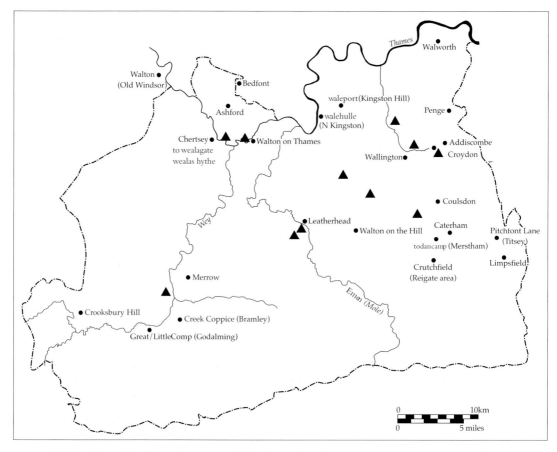

84 Location of significant place-names. Triangles mark early Saxon cemeteries. *Drawing: Audrey Graham and author, cemeteries after Poulton 1987, fig 8.1*

southern approaches to the city. It is interesting to note the parallel with the much later nineteenth century forts making a ring rather further out.

The evidence from place-names can add to the picture, but it must be used with care as it is open to differing interpretations. The names were not of course recorded until quite some time after our period, but some are held to be early on philological grounds. Firstly, we have names that include the Saxon word for a Briton: *wealh*. Some of these names are linked to words for a settlement: Walworth, just south of Southwark; Wallington; Walton on Thames *(84)*. A lost Walton at Old Windsor, only just over the border into Berkshire, should also be noted. *Wealh* sometimes also has the meaning ' (British) slave' , but it is difficult to see how a place could have gained the name ' farm of the slave(s)' and place-name experts generally agree that in these names the meaning should be 'Briton'. The place-name Walton on the Hill is not usually accepted as including *wealh*, but the rule depends on early versions of the name having a surviving medial e (eg Waletone). In fact there are several mixed with others not having the e; alternative derivations are suggested from *weall* = 'wall' or *weald* = 'forest'. The first is unlikely; a building would be recognised in some way as such and *weall* does not seem to be used in this way, while any other stone wall is unlikely in Surrey. 'Forest' makes greater sense as there is an extensive area of Clay with Flints next to Walton on the Hill, but surface deposits mask a lot of it and the Walton Heath villa is set in the middle, implying a cleared area. With this in mind, and in view of the fact that the parish has not one Roman villa but two, Walton derived from *wealh* should not be ruled out in this case.

More important are two other groups of minor names, at Kingston and Chertsey respectively. The Kingston names are *waleport* in the area of the probable settlement on Kingston Hill, and *walehulle* near the Thames just to the north of the town. Chertsey's Saxon charter bounds give us *to wealagate* ('gate of the British') and *wealas hythe* ('landing place of the British'). To this evidence for Britons may be added Chertsey itself, 'the island of Cerotus', whose name is British (it is related to Caratacus), and Ashford in Middlesex, not far to the north of Chertsey. This was originally 'Echel's ford', including another probably British name. We might note in passing that a priest acting as a witness to the grant of land for a minster at Farnham, made by Ceadwalla of Wessex in about AD 685, was named Welisc, which is derived from *wealh*. Ceadwalla's own name is British and he had a half brother Mul (possibly 'half-breed', ie having British and Saxon parentage). Molesey, not far from Walton on Thames, means 'the island of Mul', although there is no reason to assume that they are the same person.

Other names also enter the equation: Penge, some 9km to the south of Walworth (and about 5km north of Croydon) has a wholly British name (*pen* + *coed*, meaning something like 'chief wood'). In the late Saxon period it was a large wood or swine pasture attached to Battersea and forming a detached part of the parish; perhaps this echoes a much earlier land holding. Leatherhead and Merrow are also held to have wholly British names, while Coulsdon, Limpsfield, Crutchfield (Reigate Hundred), Creek Coppice in Bramley and Crooksbury Hill have names which are partly Brittonic. The first element of Caterham is thought to be an ancient formation. The names of the three main rivers are also ancient survivals: Thames, Wey and Emen (the old name for the Mole; the modern name is a back formation from Molesey).

These names must indicate some degree of contact between Saxon and Briton, and other names are also suggestive: the Latin word *crocus* seems to be the significant element in the name Croydon (discussed above) and Addiscombe nearby includes the word *camp*, derived from Latin *campus*, with some sort of field-related meaning. This word also turns up in the bounds of Merstham and there is a cluster of related names around the Darenth valley in West Kent. An isolated example may be indicated by the field names Great and

Little Comp in Godalming. The element *funta* is also taken from Latin (*fontana*) and must indicate a special Roman period spring or well, presumably one thought to have been provided with a stone surround or piped in some way: Bedfont, just to the north of Ashford, is one of the few British examples; it is probable that Pitchfont Lane, right next to the Titsey villa, is another.

Place-name scholars have been struck by the relative frequency of names referring to Britons or including British elements in Surrey. These names indicate the presence of Britons at significant places round the great loop of the Thames from Kingston to Walton to Chertsey to Windsor, and also cluster around to the south of London in the Walworth–Penge–Croydon area *(84)*. Both are also areas with early Saxon cemeteries. The conclusion seems reasonable that here we have evidence for early contact between Saxons and Britons and some sort of coexistence. It may even be that these names mark the edges of areas of British occupation. If to this we add evidence such as the late seventh-century laws of Wessex, which specifically recognised Britons, both free and slave, it seems clear that we must allow for some element of British survival in Surrey, even in the area of the earliest Saxon settlement. Other parts of the county may have remained more wholly British, becoming more 'Saxon' in due course by a process of cultural assimilation and by later land grabbing by the dominant rulers (represented by later Saxon cemeteries at places like Leatherhead and Guildford). A picture in which the Britons were wholly replaced by Saxons simply does not accord with the evidence we have at present. Although we cannot trace Britons in the archaeological record, it may well be that with the breakdown of Roman-period material culture the surviving Britons took up the styles of pottery and metalwork of the incomers. There is already a recognised intermingling of Roman and Germanic styles in later Roman metalwork, and pottery vessels showing the influence of one style or the other.

A plausible story about the end of Roman Surrey would start with the uncertainties of the late Roman period leading to some abandonment of sites and perhaps people fleeing to the supposed protection of the city. Although it has been claimed that late Roman London was a 'garden city' with stone buildings standing in large open areas this seems unlikely; the city had one of the largest walled areas in the western Empire, some of the late cemeteries are crowded and apparently poor and the amphitheatre was evidently kept in order until late. The remnants of the provincial field army were withdrawn in AD 407 to support the self-styled Constantine III in a bid for power in Gaul. This is often represented as the Romans leaving the Britons to their fate, but the irony is that the field army would have been largely German and the Britons were now all formally Romans (the status of Roman citizen had been granted to free people throughout the Empire many years previously). The remaining British authorities took steps to employ others to fill the vacuum and in due course groups of 'Saxons' were established to protect the southern approaches to London.

'Saxon' to a late Roman Briton may have meant something like 'English' did to a southern Frenchman in the fourteenth century: a raider best avoided (these 'English' were more or less part of the English army but were often a variety of nationalities anything but English). As their burial rites show, the Germanic peoples occupying areas like Surrey were a rather mixed bunch. Some of these people wandered a lot before settling; for example there were Saxons with the Lombards in Italy. Bands came together for mutual advantage, and probably included some Britons as well: there are rulers of Wessex with British names. This was clearly a time when being handy with a sword (indeed having one) was a good employment prospect, whoever you were. The Saxon name may later have been worn with pride when a kingdom of some sort was established and the need for a royal ancestry and some sort of group identity became paramount.

A final point of interest is the county's name. It means something like the 'southern district' and includes an archaic Saxon element *-ge*, related to the German word *Gau*. Surrey may therefore have gained its name from the group of early Saxon settlements south of London, for the 'southern district' must have been south of something of importance. This would be fitting in view of the close links between London and Surrey ever since the city was founded at the start of the Roman period.

AFTERWORD

Oddly enough, Surrey had a starring role in the film *Gladiator*, standing in for the northern frontier of the Empire. The film is an example of how the Romans continue to fascinate. In Surrey, Roman altars from Hadrian's Wall were used in eighteenth-century landscaping at places like Busbridge, near Godalming; there were 'Roman' temples, a mausoleum and a bath-house at Painshill Park; an 'amphitheatre' (really a theatre) at Claremont; we even have columns from Leptis Magna in Libya, at the Virginia Water lake. But this interest in things Roman leads to a distorted image of Roman Britain in people's minds, with overmuch emphasis on the 'Roman'. There are even archaeologists who try to ignore the Roman period as though it was an anomaly in British history, as though the 'Romans' invaded in AD 43 and left again not long before AD 410, still legionaries in their fancy uniforms. I hope that anyone reading this book will have been able to see that this picture is quite false; most of the people, most of the time, in Roman Surrey were indigenous, and their story is part of the continuing process of the history of our county and our island.

There is still very much to learn and much of the evidence has been lost so what is left is very important: our archaeological resource must be managed with care. Archaeology is a constant process of discovery and reinterpretation, but it is possible to outline some key areas currently in need of far more information: the nature of settlements like Ewell; animals and crops; land use and landscape; woodland management; rural occupation sites; villa estates; *civitas* links; pottery supply; comparative coin loss patterns; burials; the transition from

85 Tabard Square, Southwark: marble plaque dedicated to the god Mars Camulos and the 'spirits' of the emperors by Tiberinius Celerianus of the Bellovaci, *moritix* of London, perhaps around AD 160 (about 29 x 32cm). *Courtesy Pre-Construct Archaeology*

Iron Age to Roman; changes across the period; the transition from Roman to Saxon. Recent discoveries like those at Tabard Square *(85)*, Carshalton *(46)*, Wanborough *(75)* and Frensham *(78)* illustrate the potential.

FURTHER READING
AND REFERENCES

A book of this kind is based on a very large number of other published works. Those who wish to pursue Roman Surrey in more detail will find most of the references they need in the following papers, full details of which are given in the bibliography: Bird 1987; 1996; 2000; 2004a. For a survey of the wider south-east in the Roman period, see Rudling 1988. For Surrey's archaeology in general see Bird & Bird 1987 and Cotton et al 2004. New information appears regularly in *Surrey Archaeological Collections*, the journal of Surrey Archaeological Society, including a round-up of the results of fieldwork throughout the area covered by this book.

For Iron Age Surrey: Hanworth 1987 and Poulton 2004
For Caesar to Claudius: Creighton 2000
For the debate about the invasion: Bird 2002 and the references given there.
For the Atrebates: Henig 2002
For roads: Margary 1956
For Southwark: Sheldon 2000
For Staines: Jones & Poulton forthcoming and McKinley forthcoming
For tiles: Brodribb 1987 and Betts et al 1994
For pottery: Tyers 1996
For religion: Bird 2004b and the references given there
For Saxon Surrey: Poulton 1987 and Hines 2004

BIBLIOGRAPHY

The bibliography provides the references for the illustrations, for the quotations and for the further reading section.

Abdy, C., & Bierton, G., 1997 'A gazetteer of Romano-British archaeological sites in Ewell', *Surrey Archaeological Collections*, **84**, 123-141

Adkins, L., & Adkins, R., 1984 'Two Roman coffins from near St Mary's Church, Beddington', *Surrey Archaeological Collections*, **75**, 281-4

Adkins, L., Adkins, R.A., & Perry, J.G., 1987 'Excavations at Beddington 1984-87: the final interim', *London Archaeologist*, **5.13**, 349-52

Betts, I., Black, E.W., & Gower, J., 1994 *A corpus of relief-patterned tiles in Roman Britain*, Journal of Roman Pottery Studies, **7**

Bidder, H.F., & Morris, J., 1959 'The Anglo-Saxon cemetery at Mitcham', *Surrey Archaeological Collections*, **56**, 51-131

Bird, D.G., 1987 'The Romano-British period', in Bird & Bird 1987, 165-96

Bird, D.G., 1996 'The London region in the Roman period', in Bird et al 1996, 217-32

Bird, D.G., 2000 'The environs of Londinium: roads, roadside settlements and the countryside', in Haynes et al 2000, 151-174

Bird, D.G., 2002 'The events of A.D. 43: further reflections', *Britannia*, **33**, 257-263

Bird, D.G., 2004a 'Surrey in the Roman period: a survey of recent discoveries', in Cotton et al 2004, 65-76

Bird, D.G., 2004b 'Roman religious sites in the landscape', in Cotton et al 2004, 77-90

Bird, J., & Bird, D.G. (eds), 1987 *The archaeology of Surrey to 1540.* Surrey Archaeological Society

Bird, J., Hassall M., & Sheldon, H. (eds), 1996 *Interpreting Roman London. Papers in memory of Hugh Chapman*, Oxbow Monograph **58**

Brodribb, G., 1987 *Roman brick and tile*

Clark, A.J., 1949 (1950) 'The fourth-century Romano-British pottery kilns at Overwey, Tilford', *Surrey Archaeological Collections*, **51**, 29-56

Cooper, T.S, ed J.L. Gower and M Gower, 1984 'The Roman villa at Whitebeech, Chiddingfold: excavations in 1888 and subsequently', *Surrey Archaeological Collections*, **75**, 57-83

Cotton, J., Crocker, G, & Graham, A. (eds), 2004 *Aspects of archaeology and history in Surrey: towards a research framework for the county*, Surrey Archaeological Society

Creighton, J., 2000 *Coins and power in late Iron Age Britain*

Darwin, C., 1888 *The formation of vegetable mould through the action of worms, with observations on their habits*

Diamond, H.W., 1847 'Account of wells or pits, containing Roman remains, discovered at Ewell in Surrey', *Archaeologia*, **32**, 451-5

Falkner, H., 1907 'Discovery of ancient pottery near Farnham in 1906', *Surrey Archaeological Collections*, **20**, 228-32

Goodchild, R.G., 1937 'The Roman brickworks at Wykehurst Farm in the parish of Cranleigh. With a note on a Roman tile kiln at Horton, Epsom', *Surrey Archaeological Collections*, **45**, 74-96

Hampton, J.N., 1996 'Chelsham, a 'new' Roman villa', *Surrey Archaeological Collections*, **83**, 244

Hanworth, R., 1968 'The Roman villa at Rapsley, Ewhurst', *Surrey Archaeological Collections*, **65**, 1-70

Hanworth, R., 1987 'The Iron Age in Surrey', in Bird & Bird 1987, 139-164

Hayman, G., 1997 'The excavation of two medieval pottery kiln sites and two sections through the London–Lewes Roman road at Clacket Lane, near Titsey, 1992', *Surrey Archaeological Collections*, **84**, 1-87

Hayman, G., 1998 'Excavation in St Martin's Walk, Dorking', *Surrey Archaeological Collections*, **85**, 63-95

Haynes, I., Sheldon, H., and Hannigan, L. (eds), 2000 *London under ground. The archaeology of a city*

Henig, M, 2002 *The heirs of King Verica. Culture and politics in Roman Britain*

Hines, J, 2004 'Suþre-gē — the foundations of Surrey', in Cotton et al 2004, 91-102

Jackson, R., 1996 'A new collyrium-stamp from Staines and some thoughts on eye medicine in Roman London and Britannia', in Bird et al 1996, 177-87

Jones, P., 1982, 'Saxon and early medieval Staines', *Transactions of the London and Middlesex Archaeological Society*, **33**, 186-213

Jones, P., & Poulton, R,. forthcoming, *Excavations in the Roman and medieval town of Staines*

Leveson-Gower, G., 1869 'On a Roman villa discovered at Titsey', *Surrey Archaeological Collections*, **4**, 214–37

Lowther, A.W.G., 1930 'Excavations at Ashtead, Surrey. Third report (1929)', *Surrey Archaeological Collections*, **38.2**, 132–48

Lowther, A.W.G., 1949 (1950) 'Roman villa at Sandilands Road, Walton on the Hill. Excavations of 1948-9', *Surrey Archaeological Collections*, **51**, 65–81

Lowther, A.W.G., 1953-4 (1955) 'Report on the excavation, 1946-7, of a Roman site at Farnham, Surrey', *Surrey Archaeological Collections*, **54**, 47–57

Margary, I.D., 1956 *Roman Ways in the Weald*, third edition

McKinley, J., forthcoming 'Welcome to Pontibus ... gateway to the west', *Surrey Archaeological Collections*

Pocock, W.W., 1864 'Roman pavement etc upon Walton Heath', *Surrey Archaeological Collections*, **2**, 1–13

Poulton, R., 1987 'Saxon Surrey', in Bird & Bird 1987, 197–222

Poulton, R., 2004 'Iron Age Surrey', in Cotton et al 2004, 51–64

Radice, B. (trans), 1963 *The letters of the Younger Pliny*

Rudling, D., 1988 'A colony of Rome, AD 43-410', in P. Drewett, D. Rudling & M. Gardiner, *The south-east to AD 1000*, 178–245

Sheldon, H., 2000 'Roman Southwark', in Haynes et al 2000, 121–150

Stephenson, M, 1915 'A Roman building found at Compton', *Surrey Archaeological Collections*, **28**, 41–50

Smith, J.T., 1980 'The Roman villa at Rapsley: an interpretation', *Surrey Archaeological Collections*, **72**, 63–8

Stamp, L.D., & Willatts, E.C., 1942 *Part 81: Surrey*, L.D. Stamp (ed) The Land of Britain: the report of the Land Utilisation Survey of Britain

Tomlin, R.S.O., 1996 'A five acre wood in Roman Kent', in Bird et al 1996, 209–215

Tyers, P.A., 1996 *Roman pottery in Britain*

Woodcock, G. (ed), 1967, *William Cobbett. Rural rides*

LIST OF ILLUSTRATIONS

BLACK AND WHITE FIGURES

COLOUR PLATES

INDEX

If you are interested in purchasing other books published by Tempus, or in case you have difficulty finding any Tempus books in your local bookshop, you can also place orders directly through our website

www.tempus-publishing.com